AMAZING
EVOLUTION

The Journey of Life

Anna Claybourne

Illustrated by
Wesley Robins

IVY KIDS

CONTENTS

INTRODUCTION

We live in a world where everything changes. Rocks slowly crack, crumble away, and form again. Cliffs, valleys and beaches change shape. The planets and stars themselves move and change.

Most of all, and fastest of all, living things change. They change from one season to the next. They are born, grow, get old and die. And they have babies, so as they die, their babies replace them. And over the generations, new types of living things develop, or evolve.

This process, called evolution, is very important. It's a big part of biology, the study of living things. Scientists only discovered how evolution works in the 1800s – less than 200 years ago. They are still studying it to find out more.

• Evolution explains how all the living things on Earth today came to be here.

• It's the reason why there are so many different types, or species, of living things.

• It's because of evolution that living things seem so well-suited, or adapted, to their surroundings.

• Evolution also explains why there used to be many other creatures, such as the dinosaurs, which no longer exist.

• It's thanks to evolution that we humans are here too. And, like other living things, we are still evolving.

Evolution is an amazing, ever-changing process. This book explores what it is, how it works, and who discovered its secrets. It shows how life has changed and branched out into so many different forms over billions of years, and reveals how we humans are related to all living things – not just apes and monkeys, but cats, dogs, fish and even bananas! You'll meet some of the strangest and most incredible creatures and features that evolution has brought into existence, and discover where evolution might be headed in the future.

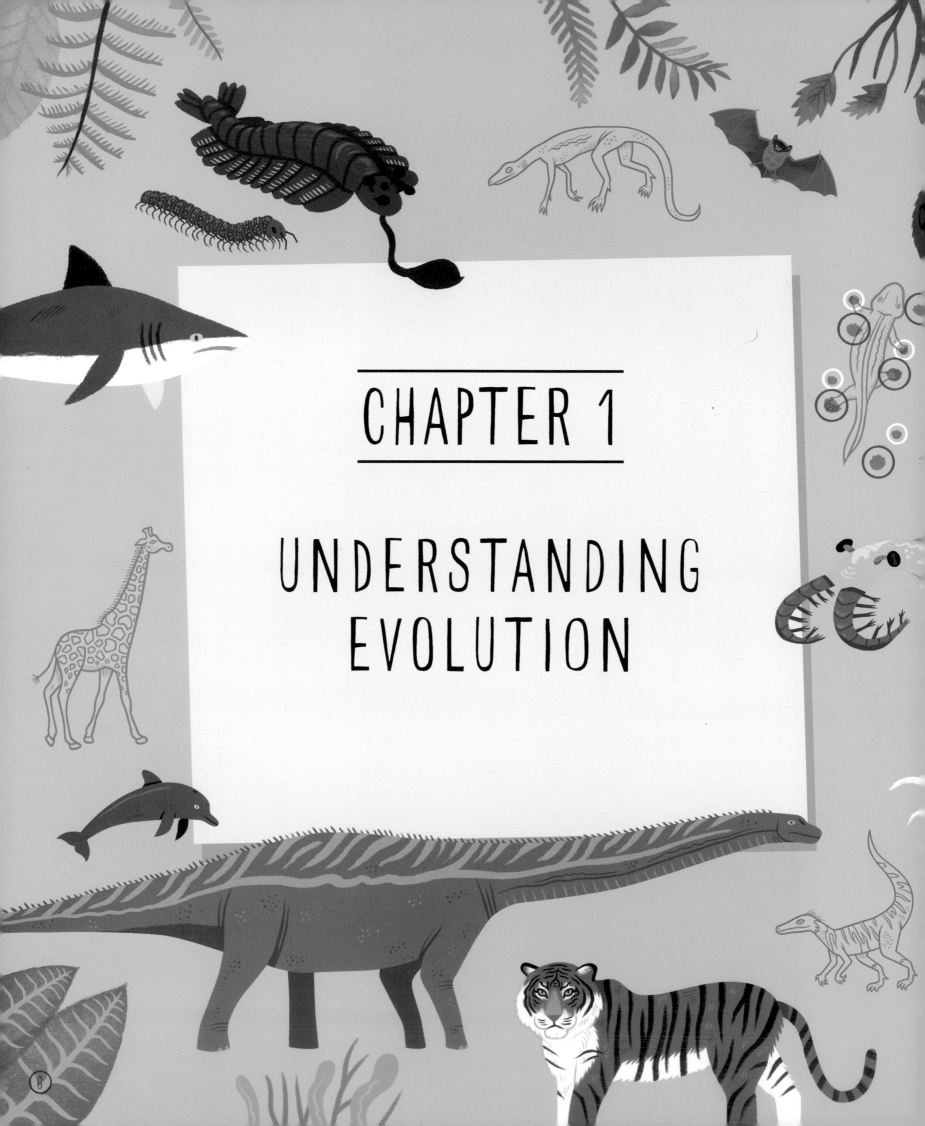

CHAPTER 1

UNDERSTANDING EVOLUTION

Our planet is bursting with life. From the deep oceans teeming with plankton, fish, jellyfish, whales and dolphins, to the vast green grasslands and forests stretching across continents, to the biggest modern cities, home to millions of human beings – there are living things almost everywhere. But if you could travel four billion years back in time, there wouldn't be any of this. Between then and now, something amazing happened: life somehow began, and evolved into many different forms.

For a long time, no one really knew how this could have happened, and how it worked. It was only in the 1800s that scientists began to understand the evolution of living things, what causes it, and how it works. Ever since, it has been one of the most important topics in science.

WHAT IS EVOLUTION?

Evolution is the way that living things have changed, and keep changing, over time. Each type, or species, of living thing has evolved to be the way it is now and that's why there are so many different, amazing kinds of life on Earth. Evolution is what has allowed these species to change, live in different places, find their food in different ways, and end up looking so different from each other.

STORIES IN THE STONE

Fossils dug up from the ground show us some of the ways living things have changed over time. We have dragonflies today, but fossils show that 300 million years ago, there were dragonflies that were much, much bigger!

The enormous *Meganeura* dragonfly had a wingspan of up to 70 cm.

Dinosaurs roamed Earth 150 million years ago. We know this because of the fossils that have been found. There are no dinosaurs today, but some types of dinosaurs evolved into birds, which do still exist.

Dinosaurs are believed to be the ancestors of birds, and some had feathers and beak-like mouths.

FROM ONE TO MANY

Scientists think that life on Earth began with just one type of simple, single-celled living thing, perhaps around 3.8 billion (3,800 million) years ago. From this first life form, gradual changes led to more and more changes and billions of different species – all the creatures that have ever lived, and all the living things on Earth today. As time goes on, living things continue to change and evolve. Evolution is never 'finished'. It's still happening now.

- THE EVOLUTION OF US -

In this timeline, you can see some of the stages in the evolution of humans from the first single-celled living things. It does not show all of evolution – it's just one of millions and millions of pathways, leading to all the different species that exist, and have existed in the past.

The abbreviation for 'million years ago' is mya.

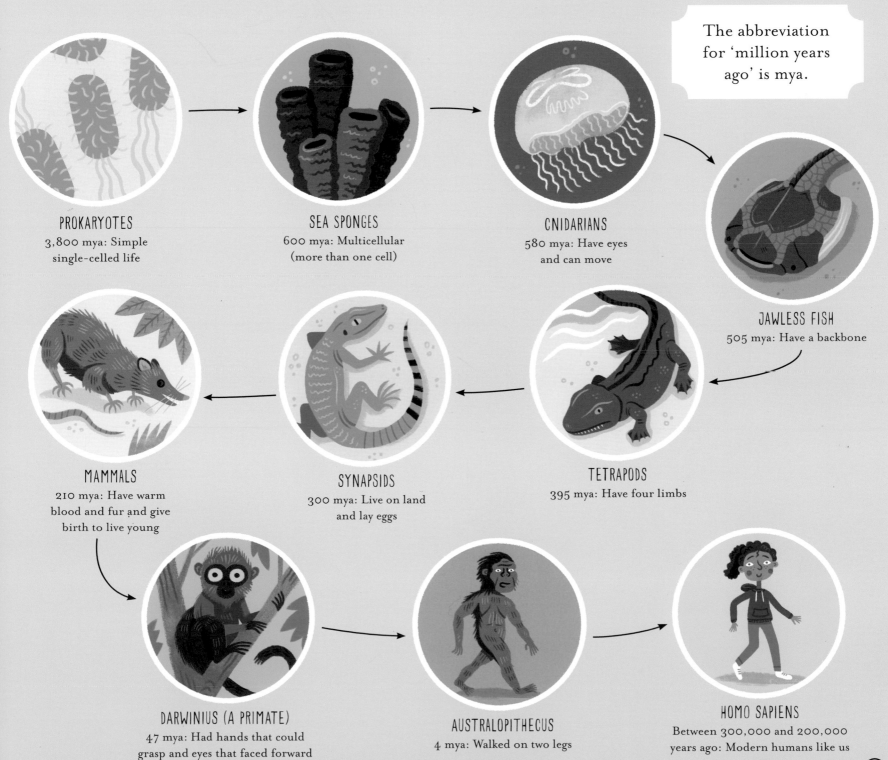

PROKARYOTES
3,800 mya: Simple single-celled life

SEA SPONGES
600 mya: Multicellular (more than one cell)

CNIDARIANS
580 mya: Have eyes and can move

JAWLESS FISH
505 mya: Have a backbone

MAMMALS
210 mya: Have warm blood and fur and give birth to live young

SYNAPSIDS
300 mya: Live on land and lay eggs

TETRAPODS
395 mya: Have four limbs

DARWINIUS (A PRIMATE)
47 mya: Had hands that could grasp and eyes that faced forward

AUSTRALOPITHECUS
4 mya: Walked on two legs

HOMO SAPIENS
Between 300,000 and 200,000 years ago: Modern humans like us

THE VARIETY OF LIFE

Our planet, Earth, is the only place we know of where life exists. On all our explorations into space, we haven't found life anywhere else. Aliens from other worlds have never contacted us – so far, that is! But here on our own planet, we don't have just one kind of life, or just a few kinds. Our world is home to MILLIONS of different species.

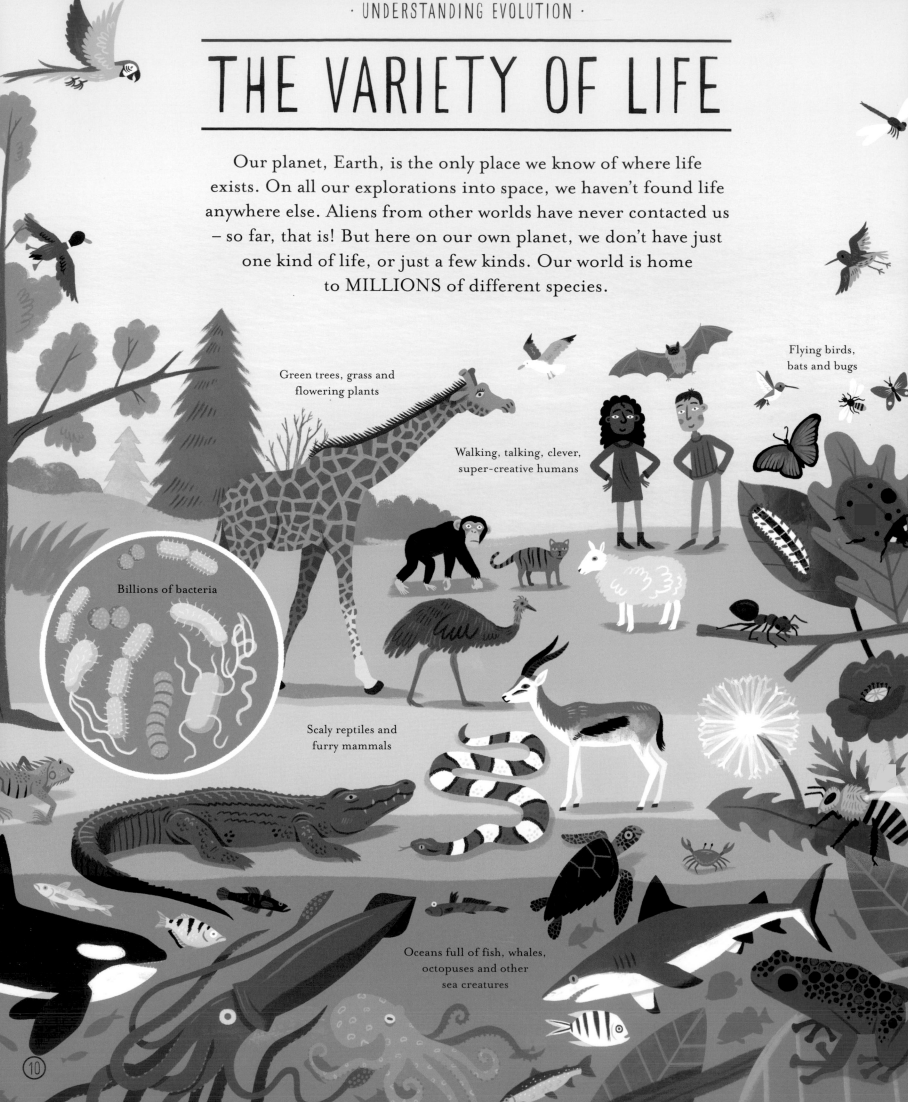

Green trees, grass and flowering plants

Flying birds, bats and bugs

Walking, talking, clever, super-creative humans

Billions of bacteria

Scaly reptiles and furry mammals

Oceans full of fish, whales, octopuses and other sea creatures

PERFECTLY SUITED

Almost everywhere in the world, there are living things. They are usually brilliantly well-suited to the places they live in, and the food they can find to eat.

The anglerfish lives deep down in the sea, where it's pitch dark. It has a lighting-up lure on its head, to attract smaller fish and shrimps towards it.

But you wouldn't find this fish in shallow, sunny waters. Its features would not be as useful there.

In the shallow coastal waters off southern Australia lives a very different fish, the leafy seadragon. Its leafy shape and colour gives it amazing camouflage among the reefs and seaweed-covered rocks. But in the deep sea, this disguise would not help it to survive. There is not enough sunlight down there for leafy plants to grow.

WEIRD AND WONDERFUL

Some creatures have bizarre features that we still can't explain. The Brazilian treehopper is one. It has an unusual set of spheres on its head, making it look like a very strange helicopter. No one is sure what they're for!

HOW DID IT HAPPEN?

For a long time, the variety of life on Earth was a big puzzle for scientists. They wondered:

Why are there so many different types of living things?

Why were they different in the past?

Did living things change from one species into another? How could that happen?

Then, in the middle of the 1800s, two great thinkers came up with the answer. They were Charles Darwin and Alfred Russel Wallace.

Long-eared bat   Scarab beetle   Trilobite fossil   Lobe-finned fish   Tetrapod

DARWIN AND WALLACE

The early 1800s was a boom time for science. Batteries, motors and steam trains were invented. People began to dig up fossils and ancient ruins, and became very interested in the past. Scientists also discovered how Earth had changed over time.

DARWIN'S ADVENTURE

In 1809, Charles Darwin was born in Shrewsbury, England. Though his father wanted him to become a doctor, his real passion was nature. He spent his time spotting and collecting wildlife. When he was 22, thanks to a friend's recommendation, Darwin began a five-year, round-the-world voyage, as the naturalist on a survey ship, the HMS *Beagle*. His job was to observe and collect wildlife specimens. Along the way, he studied thousands of plants, animals and fossils. This made him think about how species changed over time, and where new species came from.

In the Galápagos Islands off Ecuador in South America, Darwin found slightly different species of finch living on different islands. They seemed to have developed in different ways – but how had this happened?

Darwin saw the world's largest species of tortoise in the Galápagos Islands.

MARY ANNING

Starting in 1811, when she was only 12 years old, famous fossil hunter Mary Anning unearthed several important new fossils. Her discoveries made other scientists think more and more about living things, and why some of them seemed to have been so different in the past. Anning lived in Lyme Regis, on the English coast, where many fossils are still found to this day. She spent her life as a fossil hunter and expert. Her dog Tray helped her on her fossil-hunting trips.

This 200-million-year-old fossil of a plesiosaur (a kind of sea reptile) was one of Mary Anning's most important finds.

WALLACE'S WANDERINGS

Alfred Russel Wallace was born in Wales, UK, in 1823. Though he worked as a surveyor and teacher, Wallace, like Darwin, was a fanatical nature collector. As soon as he could, he set off to the Amazon rainforest to collect plant and animal specimens. Later he explored the Malay Archipelago in Southeast Asia. Like Darwin, his discoveries made him think about how species began, and how they changed. He noticed that different species seemed to be separated by an invisible line across the Malay Archipelago. Wallace realized this was due to the Earth's landmasses breaking up millions of years ago. Asian and Australasian species, separated by ocean, developed differently. But how did these species change over time?

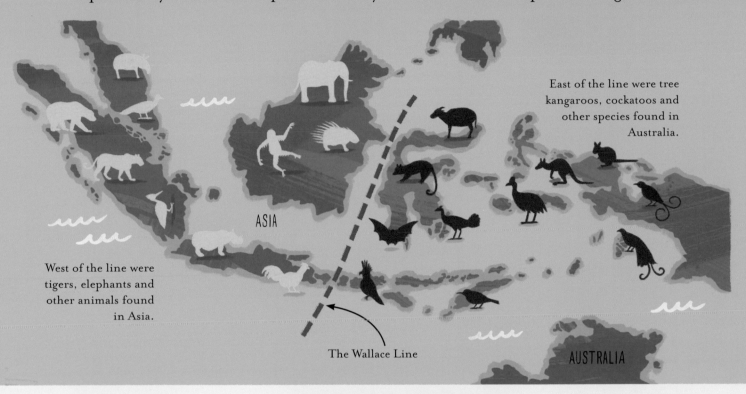

East of the line were tree kangaroos, cockatoos and other species found in Australia.

ASIA

West of the line were tigers, elephants and other animals found in Asia.

The Wallace Line

AUSTRALIA

GREAT MINDS THINK ALIKE!

After his journey, Darwin continued to study living things. In 1837, he wrote in his notebook: 'One species does change into another.' By about 1840, he had a theory of how this worked. He planned to write a book about it, but spent years collecting more notes and evidence. By 1856, Darwin and Wallace had heard about each other's interests, and were writing to each other. In 1858, while in Asia, Wallace hit upon his own explanation for how species could change. He quickly wrote it down and sent it to England. Darwin and Wallace had both come up with the same theory: natural selection.

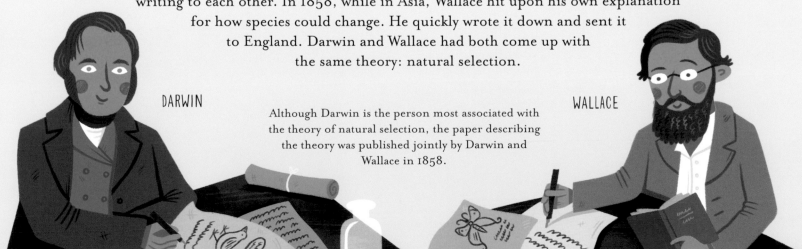

DARWIN

WALLACE

Although Darwin is the person most associated with the theory of natural selection, the paper describing the theory was published jointly by Darwin and Wallace in 1858.

THE BIG IDEA

Darwin and Wallace's theory of natural selection was presented to the world in July 1858, at a scientific meeting in London. It didn't make a big splash, though, until a year later, when Darwin published his book, *On the Origin of Species*, which made him very famous. Natural selection is still accepted as the main explanation for evolution. So, what is it? Let's think about a species of gecko, living in a shady forest.

① The geckos have a range of skin colours and textures.

YELLOWISH

BROWNISH

SMOOTH AND SHINY

ROUGH AND DULL

② The geckos hunt for insects in the forest at night. As they do so, they are hunted by predators such as birds and snakes. It's easier to find and catch geckos that are easier to see. So the predators catch more of the yellow and shiny geckos, as they reflect more moonlight. The dull, brownish geckos catch more food, too, because it's easier for them to hide.

③ More of the dull, brownish geckos survive. They live longer and have more babies. They pass on their skin type to their young.

④ This happens again and again. Over time, the species becomes mostly brown and dull. But the predators are still hungry. They still catch some geckos. The ones that look more like dead leaves are the hardest to find. These geckos survive longer, and have more babies.

⑤ Over many generations, the species starts to look more and more like a brown leaf.

THREE-PART THEORY

For evolution to work in this way, you need three things:

① VARIATION, OR DIFFERENCES

Even in the same species, there are slight differences. A litter of kittens, for example, will have different markings. The geckos have different colours and textures.

② COMPETITION FOR SURVIVAL

Not all the geckos survive – some get eaten, or can't find enough food. Nature 'selects' or chooses which ones survive, depending on which ones suit the surroundings best.

③ REPRODUCTION, OR HAVING BABIES

All living things reproduce, or make copies of themselves, such as babies or seedlings. They pass some of their features, such as shape or colour, to their young.

IT'S ALL IN THE GENES

Darwin and Wallace had discovered how evolution worked, but there were some questions they could not answer. Why is there variety between living things, even in the same species? How do living things pass on their features to their young? Now, we know that these things happen because of genes – tiny instructions inside the cells of living things. In the 1800s, microscopes were not yet powerful enough to look inside cells. No one knew how living things copied themselves. These things were only discovered later.

WHAT ARE GENES?

Genes are instructions (like a cookbook) for making chemicals called proteins, which are the building blocks of living things. Each living thing has many genes. By following the various instructions in genes, cells can grow, copy themselves, and do their jobs.

Each species has its own set of genes, called a genome. This unique genome makes that species look and act the way it does.

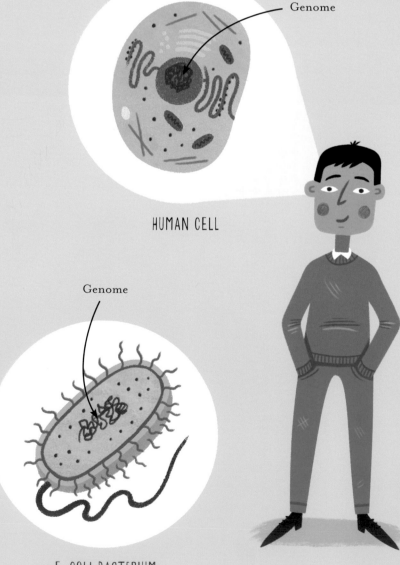

Genome

HUMAN CELL

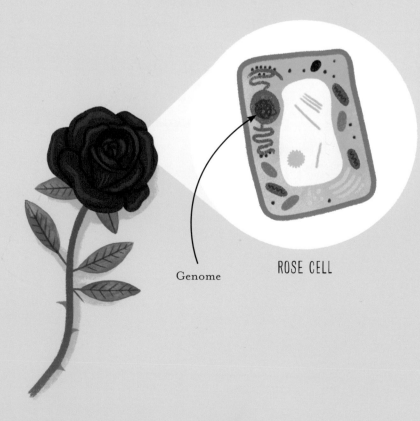

Genome

ROSE CELL

Genome

E. COLI BACTERIUM

WHAT IS DNA?

DNA is short for Deoxyribonucleic acid, a kind of long, stringy, spiral-shaped substance. DNA is what genes are made of. Each gene is a section along a long, microscopically thin string of DNA. Within the gene, proteins are arranged in patterns to make the coded instructions for the cell to follow.

Living things grow and reproduce by making copies of their cells. When cells are copied, their DNA and genes get copied, too. This is how features get passed on. So, baby giraffes are made from cells from their parents. These cells contain copies of the parents' DNA, which contain the giraffe genome. So the babies also have the giraffe genome – and turn out as giraffes!

- MAKING MUTATIONS -

When DNA is copied, it doesn't always copy exactly. There can be mistakes in the copies, called mutations, and sometimes these change how a living thing looks or works. Over time, more and more mutations cause differences between individuals. When two parents have a baby, it gets a mixture of their two genomes. Siblings (apart from identical twins) get different mixtures, or combinations, of their parents' genomes. This adds to the variety between living things, even in the same species.

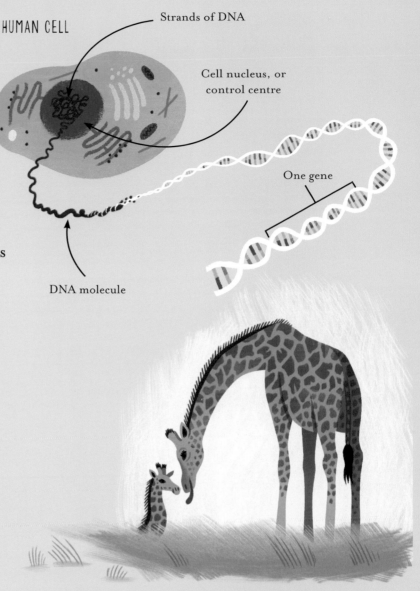

HUMAN CELL

Strands of DNA

Cell nucleus, or control centre

One gene

DNA molecule

A baby giraffe's cells contain copies of their parents' DNA, which means they become a giraffe too.

People come in many shapes and sizes. Parents pass on a mix of DNA to their children, and mutations also occur, which create differences between people.

NEW SPECIES

Darwin and Wallace were both fascinated by the question of how new species could start. That's why Darwin called his book *On the Origin of Species*. How could new species develop and branch off from older ones?

WHAT IS A SPECIES?

A species is one particular type of living thing. Scientists have discovered and named about 1.9 million species, but they are always finding new ones. They think there could be as many as 9 million altogether! Each species has its own scientific name. Members of a species can reproduce to make more living things of the same species. Usually, different species do not mate with each other.

Wallace's flying frog (*Rhacophorus nigropalmatus*) is one of almost 5,000 species of frog.

There are over 60,000 tree species, including Madagascar's giant baobab tree (*Adansonia grandidieri*).

Modern humans (*Homo sapiens*) are one of around 15,000 mammal species.

IS IT A SPECIES... OR NOT?

Some species have different varieties, called subspecies. In some cases, scientists aren't sure if a living thing really is a subspecies, or a separate species. Take giraffes, for example. Some scientists say there's only one species of giraffe, with nine subspecies. Others say there are actually eight separate giraffe species. Or six... Or four!

GIRAFFA
CAMELOPARDALIS

CAN TWO DIFFERENT SPECIES HAVE A BABY?

Sometimes, two different species can mate and have offspring, called a hybrid. The baby of a lion and a tiger is called a liger. But most hybrids cannot have their own babies, and are often unhealthy.

LIGER

HOW NEW SPECIES HAPPEN

When a new species develops, it's called 'speciation'. It usually happens when some members of a species start to evolve separately from the rest. Gradually, one species turns into two, or sometimes more.

The Grand Canyon in the USA is a deep gorge, carved by the flowing of the Colorado River. As it slowly became deeper and wider, a species of squirrel was separated into two groups, one on each side. They could no longer meet and mate. They evolved in different ways, and ended up as two species.

The Kaibab squirrel lives on the north side of the Grand Canyon.

The Abert's squirrel lives on the south side of the Grand Canyon.

- DARWIN'S FINCHES -

The finches Darwin studied (see page 12) are another example of speciation. A finch species from mainland South America spread to the Galápagos Islands. On different islands, there were different types of food. Because of natural selection, the finches on different islands evolved differently to feed on the food available. Eventually, one species became more than 10 new ones.

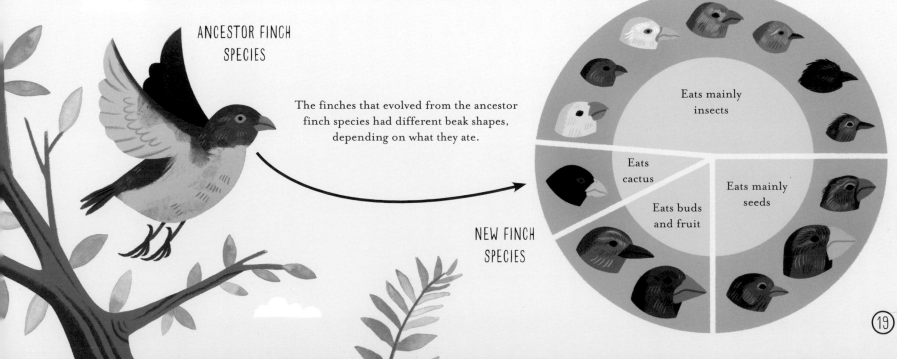

ANCESTOR FINCH SPECIES

The finches that evolved from the ancestor finch species had different beak shapes, depending on what they ate.

NEW FINCH SPECIES

Eats mainly insects

Eats cactus

Eats buds and fruit

Eats mainly seeds

GOING EXTINCT

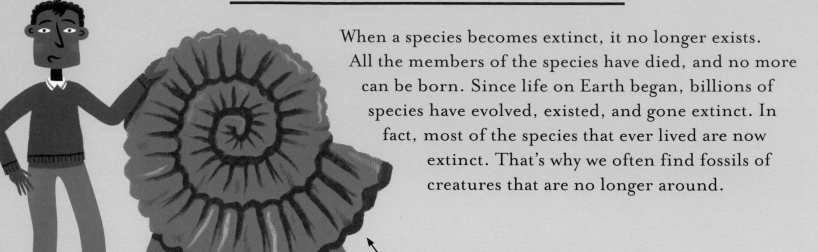

When a species becomes extinct, it no longer exists. All the members of the species have died, and no more can be born. Since life on Earth began, billions of species have evolved, existed, and gone extinct. In fact, most of the species that ever lived are now extinct. That's why we often find fossils of creatures that are no longer around.

Ammonites were sea creatures related to octopuses, with a snail-like shell. One of the largest ammonites ever found, *Parapuzosia seppenradensis*, existed from about 85 million years ago to 71 million years ago.

WAYS TO GO

There are many ways a species can become extinct:

· A species can die out if it loses its habitat – the place it lives in. For example, a forest could be destroyed by fire, or a lake could dry up.

· If the climate gets much hotter, colder, wetter or drier, some species cannot survive.

· If a species can't find enough food, it can die out.

· Disease can wipe out species.

· There's often competition between species for food or space. One takes over, while another dies out.

· Hunting or feeding by other living things can wipe out a species.

Woolly mammoths became extinct several thousand years ago, because of hunting by humans and climate change. The Earth warmed up after the last Ice Age, leading to the loss of the mammoths' habitat.

Cooksonia was a simple, early land plant. It probably died out when other plants evolved and took over.

MASS EXTINCTIONS

Sometimes, lots of species die out all at once. This is called a mass extinction. About 66 million years ago, around 80 per cent of species died out in the K-T mass extinction. It was probably caused by a big asteroid hitting Earth. Another mass extinction is happening now. It's caused by the impact of human beings on the Earth. Hunting, pollution, and destroying natural habitats to make space for cities and farmland, are driving many species to extinction.

66 mya – The dinosaurs and many other species were wiped out in the K-T mass extinction.

2012 – In the Galápagos Islands, Ecuador, the last Pinta Island tortoise, 'Lonesome George', died. His species became extinct because of hunting.

IS EXTINCTION BAD?

Many of today's extinctions are caused by humans, so we are trying to prevent them from happening. Conservation campaigns try to save endangered species such as these:

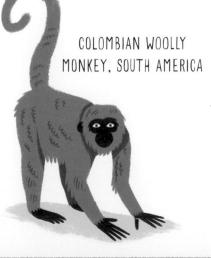

COLOMBIAN WOOLLY MONKEY, SOUTH AMERICA

AKIKIKI, HAWAII

RAFFLESIA FLOWER, SOUTHEAST ASIA

However, extinction is a natural part of evolution, too. Species do not last forever. On average, each species only survives for about 5–10 million years.

TYPES OF EVOLUTION

Natural selection (see page 14) is one of the main ways evolution happens. But it can happen in other ways, too, including sexual selection, kin selection, selective breeding and co-evolution.

CHOOSING A MATE

In some animal species, individuals choose a mate to reproduce with. A female bird might pick a male with the best song, mating dance, or colourful display of feathers. In some animal species, males fight each other, and the winner mates with the females. The fights or displays mean that the strongest or healthiest males get to mate, and pass on their genes and DNA. It's called sexual selection, because the animal is being selected as a mate, not for features that help it survive.

WILSON'S BIRD OF PARADISE

Male birds of paradise on the island of Papua New Guinea, Asia, attract the attention of female birds with elaborate dances that show off their feathers.

RED BIRD OF PARADISE

Male elephant seals fight by lunging and roaring at each other. The winner gets to mate with several females.

ALL FOR ONE AND ONE FOR ALL

Natural selection chooses the individuals that are best at surviving, and they reproduce. But what about honeybees? Only queen bees have babies. The worker bees devote themselves to helping their queen and colony survive, not themselves. Natural selection selects the colonies that are best at surviving, rather than the individuals. This is 'kin' selection, meaning family selection.

QUEEN BEE

Worker honeybees will sting, and lose their life, to defend the colony and queen.

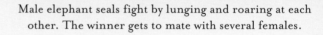

CHOOSING THE BEST

Selective breeding is a deliberate version of natural selection. Farmers have been doing it for thousands of years. Charles Darwin studied selective breeding to help him understand natural selection.

People began by farming wild plants and animals for food. They selected those with the biggest fruit, tamest nature or best taste, and used them to breed the next generation. Over many generations, this made wild plants and animals 'evolve' into more useful versions.

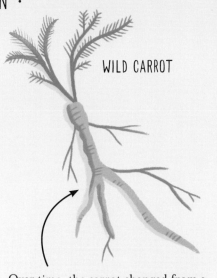

WILD CARROT

MODERN CARROT

Over time, the carrot changed from a tough, bitter root to a sweet, juicy one. People planted seeds harvested from the plants with the biggest, juiciest carrots.

From one common ancestor, over 400 dog breeds have been selectively bred to do different jobs.

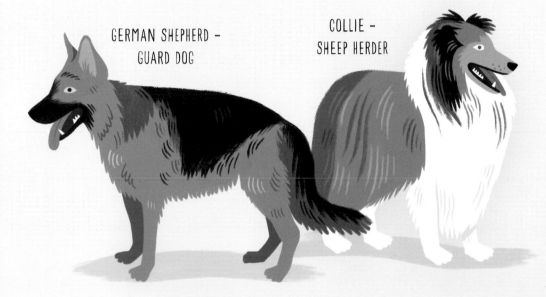

GERMAN SHEPHERD – GUARD DOG

COLLIE – SHEEP HERDER

SHIH TZU – COMPANION DOG

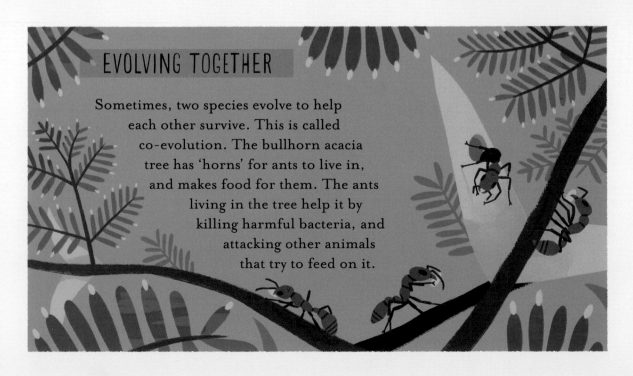

EVOLVING TOGETHER

Sometimes, two species evolve to help each other survive. This is called co-evolution. The bullhorn acacia tree has 'horns' for ants to live in, and makes food for them. The ants living in the tree help it by killing harmful bacteria, and attacking other animals that try to feed on it.

LOOKALIKES

Sometimes, two different species from different parts of the world can independently evolve to look more and more alike, but they are not closely related. Scientists call this 'convergent evolution'. The story of the southern flying squirrel and the sugar glider (on opposite page) shows how it can happen.

SAME HABITATS, DIFFERENT FAMILIES

Living things evolve to adapt to their surroundings, or habitats. For example, a forest animal might evolve to be good at climbing trees. Some types of habitats, such as forests, are found in many different parts of the world. Wherever these habitats are, living things will adapt to survive in them.

However, different parts of the world are home to different types of living things. In North America, wild mammals are 'placental', meaning their babies grow in their wombs, inside their bodies. Australia, and some nearby islands, are home to a very different mammal family, the marsupials. Instead of growing inside their mother's body, marsupial babies grow inside a pouch on her underside.

NORTH AMERICA

EUROPE

ASIA

AFRICA

SOUTH AMERICA

AUSTRALASIA

Rodents, such as rats, chipmunks and beavers, are placental mammals. They are common in North America.

Kangaroos, wallabies and wombats are all types of marsupial. Marsupials are found in Australasia.

BROWN RAT

BEAVER

WOMBAT

KANGAROO AND ROO

MATCHING MAMMALS

The placental mammals of North America and the marsupial mammals of Australia belong to completely different families. Yet each group includes an animal that has evolved in almost exactly the same way to suit life in the forest: the southern flying squirrel in North America, and the sugar glider in Australia. As a result, both animals look almost the same. At first glance you might even think they were the same species.

Southern flying squirrel (*Glaucomys volans*) – a North American rodent

Both animals have grey-brown fur for keeping warm and blending in with the tree trunks.

Sugar glider (*Petaurus breviceps*) – an Australian marsupial

Both animals are nocturnal, and have big eyes for seeing at night.

Both have loose skin along their sides, which they can spread out to glide from tree to tree.

Both have hand-like paws for climbing and holding food.

Both feed on a variety of forest food, such as insects, nuts, eggs, mushrooms, fruit, seeds, flowers and tree sap and nectar.

I'VE FOUND MY NICHE!

A habitat and the living things in it are called an ecosystem. A 'niche' is a particular place in an ecosystem, in which a living thing can evolve to fit. The sugar glider and the flying squirrel have both evolved to fit the same niche, but in different parts of the world.

25

CHAPTER 2

LIFE THROUGH THE AGES

We're used to 'history' meaning the last few thousand years, since humans began writing down and recording things that happened. But scientists who study rocks, fossils and evolution deal with a much, much longer timescale, the whole history of planet Earth. It stretches back 4.5 billion years, and is usually known as geologic time or deep time. It's hard to imagine such a huge amount of time, as humans have only existed for a tiny fraction of it.

For most of its history, Earth has been home to living things. This chapter explores how life first formed, and then developed and evolved into many different forms: from simple single-celled creatures to plants, insects, fish, land animals such as dinosaurs, flying animals, and ourselves, modern humans.

EARTH'S HISTORY

This time chart shows the history of Earth, and how life evolved. It covers an incredibly long time, from when Earth first formed, up until the present day – a total of 4.5 billion years. To make this timescale easier to understand and work with, scientists divide it into smaller blocks of time, called eons, eras and periods. Even these are millions of years long – much longer than modern humans have existed on Earth.

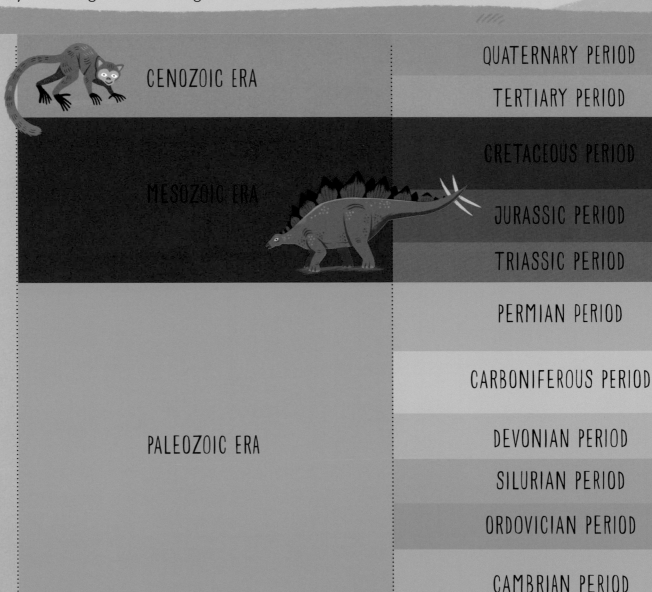

	CENOZOIC ERA	QUATERNARY PERIOD
		TERTIARY PERIOD
		CRETACEOUS PERIOD
	MESOZOIC ERA	JURASSIC PERIOD
		TRIASSIC PERIOD
PHANEROZOIC EON		PERMIAN PERIOD
		CARBONIFEROUS PERIOD
	PALEOZOIC ERA	DEVONIAN PERIOD
		SILURIAN PERIOD
		ORDOVICIAN PERIOD
		CAMBRIAN PERIOD
PROTEROZOIC EON		
ARCHAEAN EON		
HADEAN EON		

A chart like this is usually called a geological time chart, as the dates are measured by the ages of the rocks that fossils are found in.

2.5–0 MYA	Between 300,000 and 200,000 years ago – modern humans appear
66–2.5 MYA	The age of mammals. Many new mammals appear, including the first primates (our ancestors)
145–66 MYA	66 mya – the dinosaurs die out in the K-T mass extinction
199–145 MYA	Age of the dinosaurs. The first mammals and birds evolve
251–199 MYA	The first dinosaurs appear
299–251 MYA	251 mya – 95% of species become extinct in the Permian-Triassic mass extinction
359–299 MYA	First reptiles
416–359 MYA	First flying insects and amphibians
443–416 MYA	First animal life on land
488–443 MYA	First plant life on land
542–488 MYA	540 mya – The Cambrian explosion, when many new life forms develop
2,500–542 MYA	First multi-celled animals
4,000–2,500 MYA	Around 3,800 mya – the earliest simple, single-celled life appears
4,500–4,000 MYA	The eon before life began – spanning the time between the formation of Earth 4.5 billion (4,500 million) years ago, and the first life on the planet

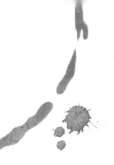

THE FOSSIL RECORD

We know about thousands of species of living things from the past – prehistoric plants, fish, dinosaurs, insects, early humans, and many more. How? It's largely thanks to fossils. Fossils are remains or imprints left in rock by living things from long ago.

HOW DO FOSSILS FORM?

When an animal or plant dies, its body usually rots away or is eaten by something. Sometimes though, if its remains are buried quickly, it may end up as a fossil. Fossils can form in different ways, but a typical fossil forms when a living thing dies and gets buried in layers of mud or sand, and its remains are slowly replaced by minerals. These are known as cast fossils.

- CAST FOSSILS -

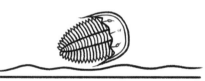

1. In a Cambrian sea, a trilobite dies and sinks to the seabed. Its soft parts rot away.

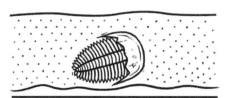

2. As layers of mud and silt settle on the seabed, the trilobite's shell slowly gets buried.

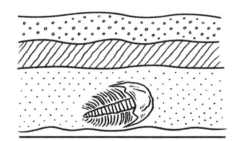

3. As more layers collect, the mud and silt gets pressed down, becoming solid rock. Water containing dissolved minerals soaks through the rock. Slowly, the trilobite shell itself dissolves, and the space it was in is filled with minerals, which become solid stone.

- TRACE FOSSILS -

Trace fossils form when marks or prints are covered by layers of mud, which eventually hardens into rock.

Dinosaur footprint, 150 million years old

- AMBER FOSSILS -

Animals and plants can be preserved in amber, which is fossilized tree sap. Millions of years ago, small insects became trapped in the sticky sap, which later hardened and formed amber.

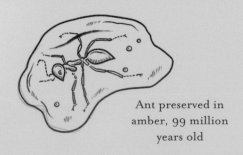

Ant preserved in amber, 99 million years old

- SOFT BODY FOSSILS -

Usually, only hard body parts like bones are fossilized. But occasionally, a creature is buried suddenly, preserving soft body parts.

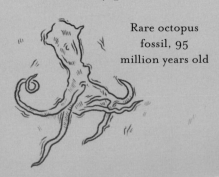

Rare octopus fossil, 95 million years old

DATES AND LAYERS

Not all rocks form in layers, but it's very common. That's why you often see stripy rocks. Different layers of rock, known as strata, are different ages. Scientists use different methods to measure how old each layer is. We can tell how long ago a species lived, from which layers of rock its fossils are found in. This history of living things, written down in rocks around the world, is called the fossil record.

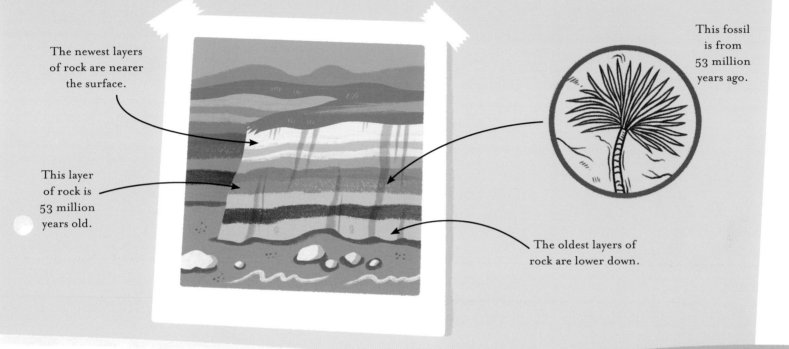

The newest layers of rock are nearer the surface.

This layer of rock is 53 million years old.

This fossil is from 53 million years ago.

The oldest layers of rock are lower down.

FINDING FOSSILS

Fossils can be revealed in several ways. Rocks are pushed upwards and form mountain ranges. As they wear down, fossils appear. At the coast, the sea wears away cliffs, revealing ancient rock layers.

Cliff falls at Lyme Regis, England, have uncovered 200-million-year-old fossils.

Sometimes, palaeontologists dig up the ground to uncover fossils.

Many dinosaur fossils have been found in North America, Argentina and China.

HOW LIFE BEGAN

For many millions of years after Earth formed, it had no life. It was much hotter than it is now, with constant volcanic eruptions and asteroid impacts. It's amazing to think that on a planet with nothing living on it, life somehow started itself. No one is sure how this happened, but scientists have several different theories.

STARTING SMALL

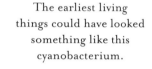

The earliest living things could have looked something like this cyanobacterium.

It's pretty certain that the first living things were tiny. A tree or even a mouse couldn't just pop into existence out of nowhere. Living things like these are made of millions of cells. Instead, the first life probably had just a single cell, like today's bacteria. The oldest fossils found so far date from around 3.8 billion years ago. They show shapes called stromatolites, flat or lumpy rock-like structures formed by single-celled, microscopic creatures.

- THE FIRST CELL -

The cell is the basic building block of all living things. A cell is made up of different molecules, held together by a skin, or membrane. To form the first, basic cell, simple molecules would have to join and react together to make the more complex ones needed for life, including DNA. Scientists think this probably happened somewhere warm and wet, as water lets chemicals move around and mix together, and heat helps them to react.

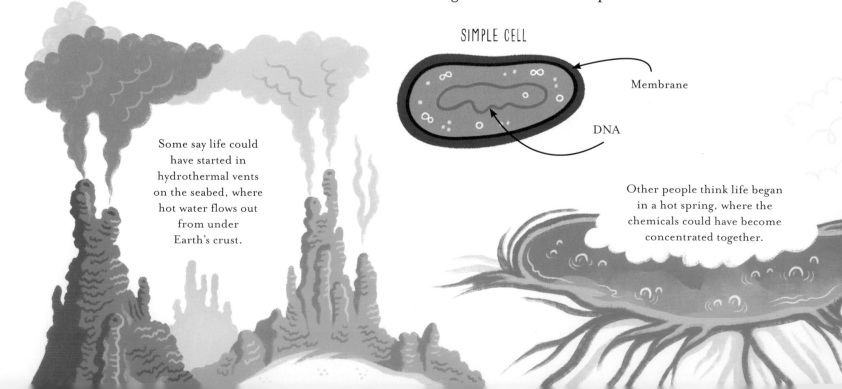

SIMPLE CELL

Membrane

DNA

Some say life could have started in hydrothermal vents on the seabed, where hot water flows out from under Earth's crust.

Other people think life began in a hot spring, where the chemicals could have become concentrated together.

LIFE IN THE WATER

Once life began, evolution could start to work, and different species developed.
For a long time, they were only found in water, not on land. By the Cambrian Period,
around 500 million years ago, there was a wide variety of sea life.

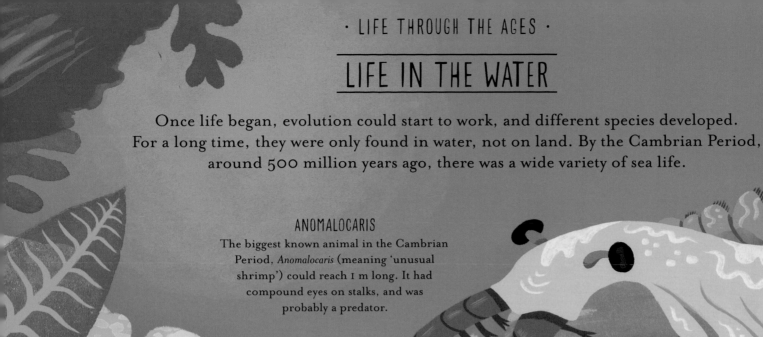

ANOMALOCARIS

The biggest known animal in the Cambrian
Period, *Anomalocaris* (meaning 'unusual
shrimp') could reach I m long. It had
compound eyes on stalks, and was
probably a predator.

JELLYFISH

The earliest jellyfish lived
in Cambrian times. They
looked similar to some
modern jellyfish.

OPABINIA

This smaller relative of
Anomalocaris had five eyes and a
long grabbing arm on its head.

TRILOBITE

Trilobites were small sea creatures related
to spiders and scorpions. They were usually
between 2 and 10 cm long.

SPONGES

Sponges are very simple animals
that stay in one place and collect
tiny bits of food from the water.

HALLUCIGENIA

Hallucigenia was a small, strange-looking
worm, only around 2.5 cm long, with
14 spines and 14 or 16 legs.

SEAWEED

Seaweeds were among the earliest
multi-celled plants.

ALIEN LIFE

According to one theory, instead of forming on
Earth, life could have come to our planet from
somewhere else, carried on a comet or asteroid.
That would mean we are all aliens!

OUT OF THE SEA

Eventually, some living things began to live on land. People often think of this as a fish with legs crawling out of the sea. Although something like this did happen, this was far from the first time living things left the water.

LAND BACTERIA

The first living things on land were probably single-celled creatures, like bacteria. They could have been washed ashore and survived in mud or on rocks, as long as 2 or 3 billion years ago. But it's hard to be sure, because microscopic fossils this old are very rare.

PLANT POWER

Next onto land came the plants, around 480 million years ago. This probably happened when simple water plants, like pond slime or seaweed, spread onto the seashore, and evolved to survive in air. They became early land plants, similar to today's mosses and liverworts.

As plants died and rotted, they created soil. They released oxygen gas, making it easier for animals to breathe air. And they provided food for animals, allowing them to live on land, too.

CREEPY-CRAWLY INVASION

Scientists think the first animals on land were small, many-legged creepy-crawlies, like insects, millipedes and centipedes. They are found in fossils up to 420 million years old. They had spiracles – holes on the sides of their bodies for breathing air. Insects and their relatives still have spiracles today.

Early land plants probably looked like today's liverworts, a type of small plant that can grow on rocks.

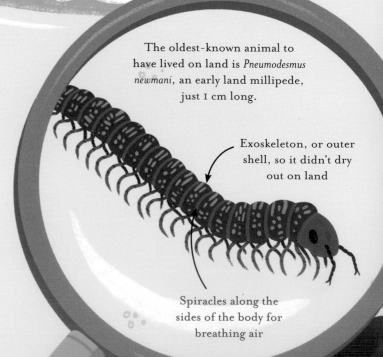

The oldest-known animal to have lived on land is *Pneumodesmus newmani*, an early land millipede, just 1 cm long.

Exoskeleton, or outer shell, so it didn't dry out on land

Spiracles along the sides of the body for breathing air

FINALLY, FISH WITH FEET

While many fish stayed in the water, others began to evolve into land animals around 395 million years ago. They developed into animals called tetrapods, meaning 'four legs'. These early tetrapods were like a cross between fish and amphibians. Some tetrapods began leaving the water, probably to find food on the shore. Tetrapods later evolved into reptiles and mammals – including humans.

TETRAPOD TRACKS

Fossilized tracks in rocks show how tetrapods crawled along on land. They also tell us how large the creatures were.

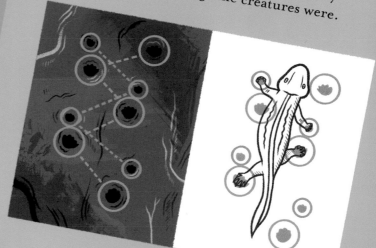

Ichthyostega was a tetrapod about 1.5 m long. It lived mostly in the water, but also spent some time on land.

Webbed toes

Fins that worked like legs

Had gills for breathing underwater, and lungs for breathing air

TODAY'S WALKING FISH

There are fish species alive today that can use their fins like feet, and live both in and out of water. The mudskipper is one – it can even climb trees!

AGE OF THE DINOSAURS

Think of prehistoric life, and you'll probably think of dinosaurs, the most famous of all fossilized creatures. Though some were small, others grew to ginormous sizes, and when people first discovered their bones, they thought they were the remains of legendary monsters and dragons.

DAWN OF THE DINOSAURS

Dinosaurs were one of the branches of living things that evolved from the four-legged, fish-like tetrapods. Unlike their relatives the lizards, dinosaurs evolved upright legs, so their bodies were lifted up above the ground.

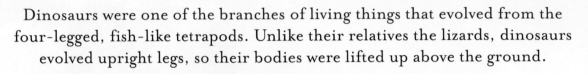

365 MYA
Early amphibians evolved from fish. *Ichthyostega* had a fish-like tail and gills, and amphibian limbs and skull.

310 MYA
Some amphibians evolved into lizard-like reptiles. The earliest known reptile was *Hylonomus*.

250 MYA
Dinosaurs evolved from a group of reptiles called archosaurs. *Lagosuchus* was an archosaur, a bit larger than a chicken.

230 MYA
The first dinosaurs, such as *Eoraptor*, lived about 230 million years ago. Eoraptor was a small meat-eating dinosaur, about the size of a dog.

Over time, dinosaurs evolved and branched out into hundreds of different species and types. There was a huge variety of different dinosaur species, with all kinds of fascinating features...

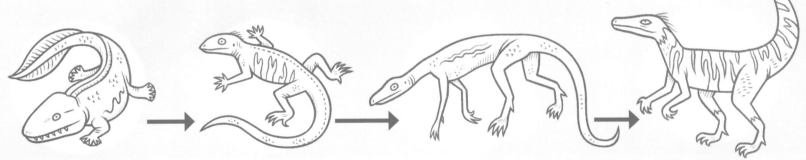

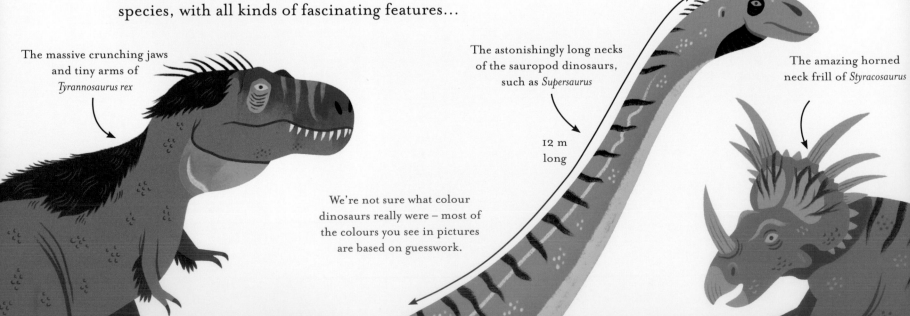

The massive crunching jaws and tiny arms of *Tyrannosaurus rex*

The astonishingly long necks of the sauropod dinosaurs, such as *Supersaurus*

12 m long

The amazing horned neck frill of *Styracosaurus*

We're not sure what colour dinosaurs really were – most of the colours you see in pictures are based on guesswork.

THE DINOSAUR AGE

Dinosaurs existed for more than 160 million years, and many different species evolved and died out at different times. Not all dinosaurs lived at the same time.

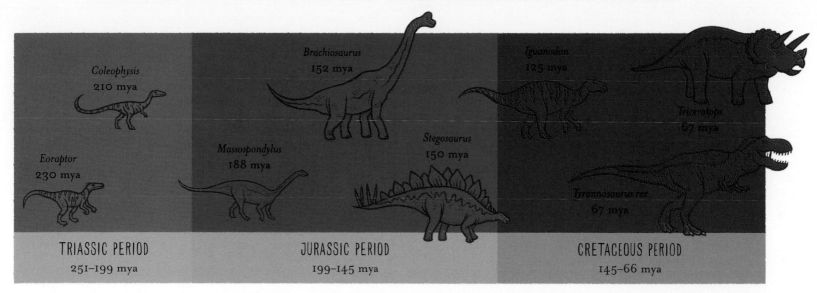

Coleophysis 210 mya	Brachiosaurus 152 mya	Iguanodon 125 mya	
Eoraptor 230 mya	Massospondylus 188 mya	Stegosaurus 150 mya	Triceratops 67 mya
			Tyrannosaurus rex 67 mya

| TRIASSIC PERIOD | JURASSIC PERIOD | CRETACEOUS PERIOD |
| 251–199 mya | 199–145 mya | 145–66 mya |

WHY DID DINOSAURS GET SO BIG?

There could be several reasons why some dinosaurs grew so big. Long-necked sauropods evolved the ability to swallow and digest lots of food without chewing it, helping them to grow bigger. Their long necks meant they could reach more food, while big bodies held in body heat. As sauropods grew bigger, some meat-eating dinosaurs evolved to get bigger too, as this allowed them to hunt and eat the sauropods.

Patagotitan was the biggest dinosaur known so far, and the biggest-ever land animal.

PATAGOTITAN:
37 m long, 70 tonnes

BLUE WHALE:
30 m long, 180 tonnes

The blue whale is still the largest animal ever. *Patagotitan* was longer, but not as heavy.

DINO DISASTER

Dinosaurs became extinct about 66 million years ago, in the K-T mass extinction, probably caused by a huge asteroid hitting Earth. After a burst of heat that killed many living things, dust would have filled the sky for years, blocking out sunlight. Many plants died, plant-eating dinosaurs starved, and so did the meat-eaters that ate them. The living things that survived were mostly smaller ones, such as small mammals, reptiles, insects, and the first birds, which had evolved from smaller dinosaurs.

RISE OF THE MAMMALS

The first mammals evolved from reptiles about 210 million years ago, and existed alongside the dinosaurs. At this time, all the biggest animals were reptiles – not just dinosaurs, but also their relatives, such as the flying pterosaurs. Mammals, meanwhile were mostly tiny. Being small, and feeding at night, helped them to avoid the dangerous dinosaurs.

MAMMALS TAKE OVER

Many mammals survived the mass extinction that wiped out the dinosaurs, 66 million years ago. As they were smaller, they didn't need as much food. They often lived in burrows, where they escaped from the heat of the asteroid strike. Later, these surviving mammals evolved and branched out to fill some of the niches once held by the reptiles.

Cute, furry *Megazostrodon* was one of the first mammals. It was about 10 cm long, and probably ate insects and other small prey.

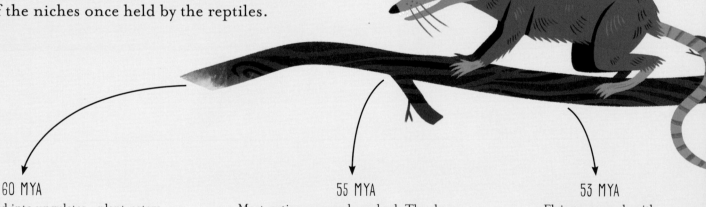

60 MYA

Some mammals evolved into ungulates – plant-eaters with hooves. They were the ancestors of modern animals such as horses, deer, hippos and giraffes.

55 MYA

Meat-eating mammals evolved. They became animals like wolves, tigers and bears.

53 MYA

Flying mammals with leathery wings evolved – the bat family.

BACK TO THE WATER

At first, all mammals were land animals. But around 52 million years ago, some groups moved back into the water, and evolved features for surviving there. As they evolved, their legs shrank away, or changed into flippers. Evolution can make features shrink or disappear, as well as develop new ones.

A modern whale's skeleton still has four limbs, like the tetrapods it evolved from, but the back limbs have almost disappeared.

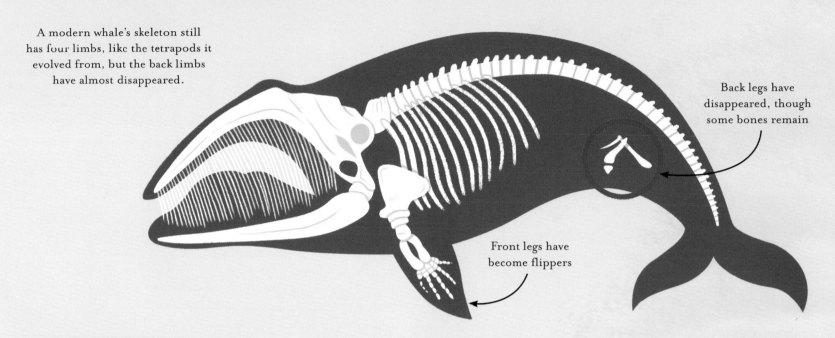

Back legs have disappeared, though some bones remain

Front legs have become flippers

Some sea mammals ended up looking similar to other sea creatures, like sharks and ichthyosaurs – another great example of convergent evolution (see page 24).

SHARK – A FISH

ICHTHYOSAUR (EXTINCT) – A REPTILE

DOLPHIN – A MAMMAL

MONSTER MAMMALS

Some prehistoric mammals were much larger than their modern relatives. They may have evolved this way to protect them from predators and help them stay warm during the last Ice Age, when Earth was much colder. But during food shortages, larger animals are more likely to die out, which might explain why these monster mammals are no longer here.

MEGATHERIUM: 6 m long

Megatherium was a giant sloth, which evolved 10 million years ago.

MODERN TWO-TOED SLOTH: Body 60–70 cm long

HERE COME THE HUMANS!

After the dinosaurs died out, a new group of mammals evolved. They were the primates, meaning 'leaders'. Scientists in the 1800s called them this because they include apes and humans, which were seen as the 'highest' or most advanced of living things. Today, the primates include lemurs, monkeys and apes.

HOW HUMANS EVOLVED

Is it true that humans are the most advanced of all living things? Well, evolution isn't a process of becoming 'higher' or more special. It just allows species to adapt to their surroundings. However, humans have turned out to be very unusual. We have the most powerful brains of any known species. And we're the only living things to have complex culture, art and technology, and written language.

The first primates developed about 55 million years ago, when some small, furry mammals evolved to live in trees. They developed hand-like feet for holding branches, and forward-facing eyes. Somewhere between 13 and 7 million years ago, apes separated into two different branches. One of these evolved into chimpanzees, and one into hominins (humans and their ancestors).

ARCHICEBUS
55 mya

The early primate *Archicebus* resembled a modern monkey, and evolved into early monkeys.

PROCONSUL
25 mya

Proconsul was like a monkey, but also had ape-like features – no tail, strong hands and a slightly human-like face.

AUSTRALOPITHECUS
4 mya

Early hominins such as *Australopithecus* evolved to walk on two legs and live on the ground.

THE HUMAN FAMILY

From early hominins such as *Australopithecus,* a family tree of humans developed, probably in Africa. One branch evolved to become *Homo sapiens,* the modern human, between 300,000 and 200,000 years ago. We know there were several species of humans, but we're not sure how they were all related. Although there's only one species of human today, as recently as 35,000 years ago, different species of humans existed together, and sometimes interacted with each other. Imagine what it would feel like to meet a different human species!

HOMO HABILIS ('HANDY HUMAN')

2.1 mya to 1.5 mya

Used stone tools
and scavenged meat.

HOMO HEIDELBERGENSIS ('HEIDELBERG HUMAN')

600,000 to 200,000 years ago

Possible ancestor of modern
humans and Neanderthals.

HOMO ERECTUS ('UPRIGHT HUMAN')

1.8 mya to 140,000 years ago

Probably the first hominin to leave
Africa. Hunter-gatherers.

HOMO NEANDERTHALENSIS ('NEANDERTHALS')

300,000 to 35,000 years ago

Our closest ancient human relatives.
Skilled tool makers and hunters.

HOMO FLORESIENSIS ('FLORES HUMAN')

100,000 to 50,000 years ago

Very short 'Hobbit' humans found
on an island in Indonesia.

WHY AREN'T WE HAIRY?

Look at our closest living relatives, chimps and gorillas, and you'll see they're much hairier than us! As humans evolved, we lost our thick body hair. There are several theories about why:

· It helped get rid of disease-carrying lice and fleas.

· It helped us keep cool while running around hunting.

· It helped us to swim in water and catch fish.

HOMO SAPIENS ('SMART HUMAN')

Between 300,000 and 200,000 years ago
to the present

Modern humans with complex brains,
advanced language, art and culture.

LUCY

We have discovered a lot about how humans have evolved from the hundreds of fossils that have been unearthed. One of the most remarkable discoveries was made in 1974, in Ethiopia, east Africa, when two palaeontologists discovered the skeleton of a hominin who lived 3.2 million years ago. 'Lucy' is not the oldest hominin fossil to have been found, but she is one of the most complete.

RECONSTRUCTING LUCY

The bone fragments that the palaeontologists found made up 40% of a skeleton. This might not sound like much, but it's actually an amazing find. Often only a tiny bit of a skeleton is found, like a rib or jawbone. As apes are symmetrical, we can see what most of the skeleton would have looked like.

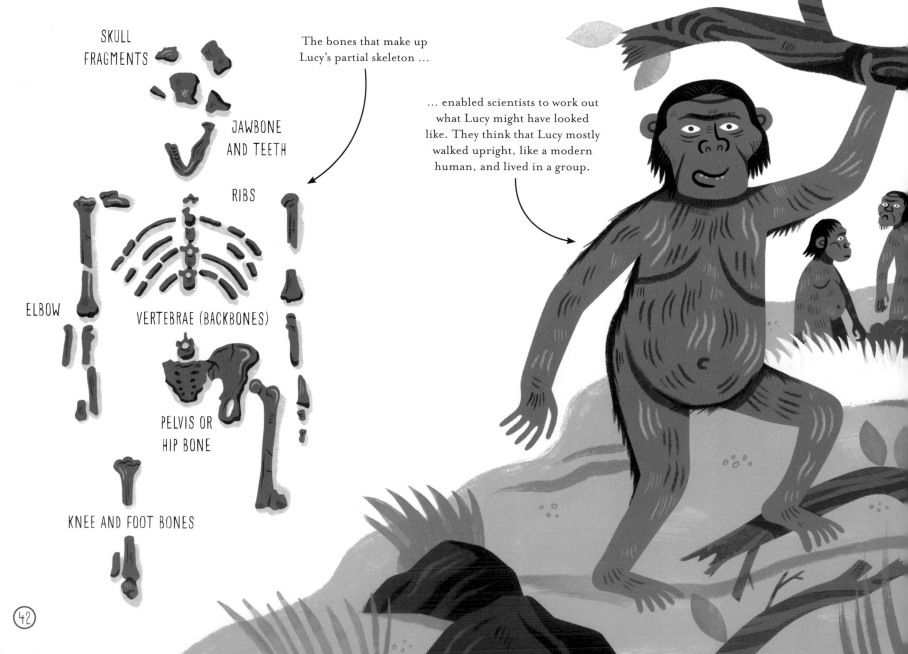

SKULL FRAGMENTS

JAWBONE AND TEETH

The bones that make up Lucy's partial skeleton …

… enabled scientists to work out what Lucy might have looked like. They think that Lucy mostly walked upright, like a modern human, and lived in a group.

RIBS

ELBOW

VERTEBRAE (BACKBONES)

PELVIS OR HIP BONE

KNEE AND FOOT BONES

CRACKING THE CLUES

By studying Lucy closely, fossil experts have found out lots more about her, and about how humans evolved. We're still not sure, though, if Lucy's species evolved directly into modern humans. However, Lucy's skeleton gives scientists lots of clues about her. The bones shown in grey are the ones that were originally found. The white bones have been added.

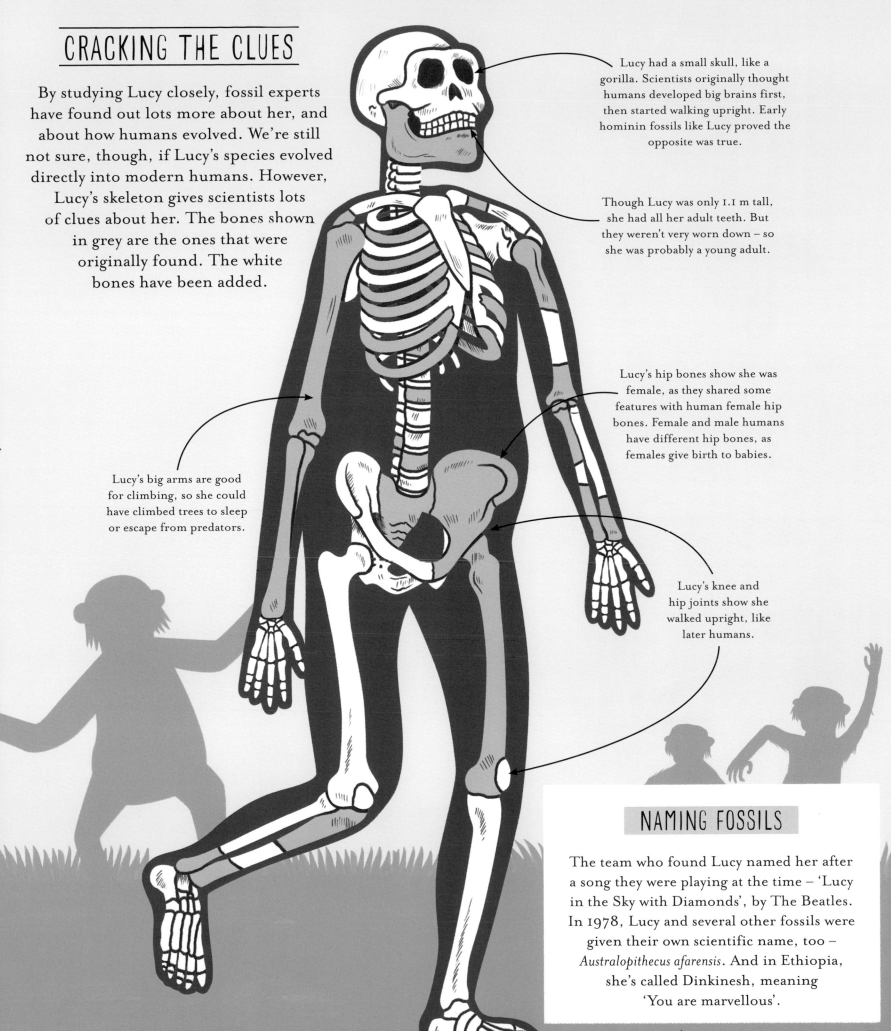

Lucy had a small skull, like a gorilla. Scientists originally thought humans developed big brains first, then started walking upright. Early hominin fossils like Lucy proved the opposite was true.

Though Lucy was only 1.1 m tall, she had all her adult teeth. But they weren't very worn down – so she was probably a young adult.

Lucy's hip bones show she was female, as they shared some features with human female hip bones. Female and male humans have different hip bones, as females give birth to babies.

Lucy's big arms are good for climbing, so she could have climbed trees to sleep or escape from predators.

Lucy's knee and hip joints show she walked upright, like later humans.

NAMING FOSSILS

The team who found Lucy named her after a song they were playing at the time – 'Lucy in the Sky with Diamonds', by The Beatles. In 1978, Lucy and several other fossils were given their own scientific name, too – *Australopithecus afarensis*. And in Ethiopia, she's called Dinkinesh, meaning 'You are marvellous'.

CHAPTER 3

THE FAMILY TREE

You might have seen a diagram of your family tree,
showing you, your parents, grandparents, cousins and
other relatives. It shows how each person is related
to the others, with lines or 'branches' of the
tree connecting them.

However, people like your cousins, grandparents and aunties
aren't your only relatives. You're also related to other animals,
like chimpanzees and gorillas. And to a pet cat, a lobster, a cow,
an anaconda, a bald eagle and even a cabbage. In fact, all of life
on Earth belongs to one enormous family. If you could trace
your family tree back far enough, right at the start you'd find
that all animals, plants and other life forms are descended from
the same ancestors – the tiny, invisible life forms
that first appeared on Earth.

ONE BIG FAMILY

Scientists think that all species evolved from one early, single-celled life form. If that's true, it means that that first living thing is your great, great, great … and billions more 'greats' … great, great, great grandparent! This living thing is known as the Last Universal Common Ancestor – or LUCA for short.

A SIMPLE BEGINNING

The idea that everything developed from one life form is quite old. Some scientists suggested it in the 1700s. When Darwin wrote his book *On the Origin of Species* in 1859, he agreed, saying: '… from so simple a beginning, endless forms most beautiful and most wonderful have been, and are being, evolved.'

More recently, scientists have studied the DNA of different living things, and found that all known species share similar DNA patterns. This means it's very likely that we all evolved from one cell. As cells and species reproduced and evolved, they copied their DNA, and passed these patterns on.

The very first cell had DNA patterns that have been copied into all of the living things that have evolved from it.

SINGLE CELL

YOU'RE HALF CABBAGE!

You share a LOT of DNA with all kinds of other living things. Around 50% of human DNA, for example, matches the DNA in a cabbage plant. Here's how much DNA we share with some other living things:

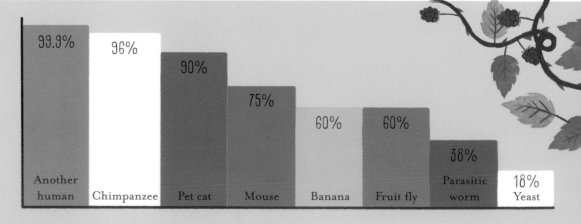

Another human	Chimpanzee	Pet cat	Mouse	Banana	Fruit fly	Parasitic worm	Yeast
99.9%	96%	90%	75%	60%	60%	38%	18%

FAMILY FEATURES

When humans evolved, we didn't evolve all our body parts and abilities from scratch. Many of them existed already, in earlier life forms. For example, our ancestors evolved four limbs around 395 million years ago, when fish moved onto land. All our ancestors since then have had four limbs. Eyes evolved even earlier, and are now found in most animals.

When a new species evolves, it sometimes develops a new feature. But usually, it adapts features that already exist. For example, as humans evolved, our skulls and brains got bigger and our legs got longer.

In fact, most vertebrates (animals with backbones) have the same basic body plan. They often have the same parts in their skeletons as we do, though they may be a different shape.

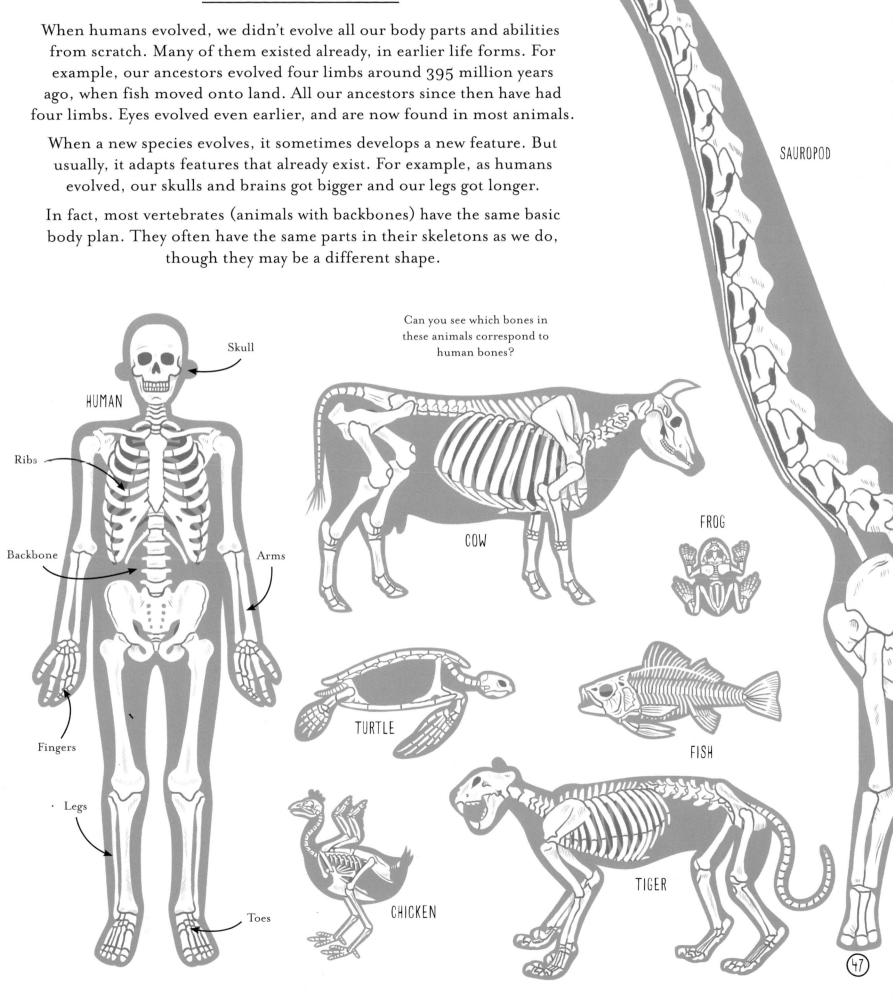

Can you see which bones in these animals correspond to human bones?

HUMAN

Skull

Ribs

Backbone

Arms

Fingers

Legs

Toes

COW

FROG

TURTLE

FISH

CHICKEN

TIGER

SAUROPOD

SHARED FEATURES: HANDS

Look at a monkey, a rat, or even a cat or a dog, and you'll see that they have body parts that resemble our hands or fingers. These parts appeared early in the evolution of vertebrates (animals with backbones).

WHAT IS A HAND?

A hand is a group of fingers, or digits, at the end of a forelimb or front limb. We usually only call it a 'hand' in humans, and animals that have similar hands, such as apes, monkeys, koalas and pandas; but many other animals have the same basic pattern. Some animals have more than five digits – for example, moles have six digits on each 'hand'. Some animals have fewer, such as birds, which have only three.

All these animals have hand-like parts, though they have evolved to look very different. Sometimes, you can only see them clearly when you look at the animal's skeleton.

HUMAN HANDS

For humans, hands are an important part of the way we have evolved. Our hands are strong, nimble and multi-functional. We can use them to pick things up, hold things, throw things, pull things, make things, write, draw and communicate. This has helped us to survive by inventing, making and building things we need, such as clothes, tools, houses and gadgets.

Our hands have opposable thumbs, meaning the thumb is opposite the fingers. This gives the hand a strong grip.

TURTLE FLIPPERS

The skeleton inside a leatherback turtle's flipper still has hand and finger parts.

WING FINGERS

The digits of bats have evolved into long, thin bones that support the animal's wings. The bat can spread them out or close them together to open or fold up its wings.

FROM LIMBS TO WINGS

In birds, the front limbs have evolved into long, thin wing bones with three digits. The bird moves its elbow, wrist and digits to fold, spread and control the wing.

MINI HANDS

Rats have hands that look like teeny human hands, Like us, they often sit up and use their 'hands' to hold things.

LOOK, NO HANDS!

Invertebrates don't have bones like ours, and don't have hands – but some of them have evolved other ways to pick up and hold things.

An octopus's arms can curl around objects, and are covered with suction cups that help it to hold on to prey.

OTTER PAWS

The sea otter's front paws have five 'fingers' inside and are very dexterous. They use stones as tools to crack open shellfish to eat. While they are sleeping, sea otters hold hands so that they don't drift apart in the water.

Crabs have powerful pincers that can seize prey and break open shells.

DARWIN'S DOODLE

When Charles Darwin was working on his theory of evolution, he wrote his ideas down in a series of notebooks. One of them contains a famous sketch, known as his 'Tree of Life' sketch. The diagram shows a line which then splits and branches off in different directions. These lines also have branches, and those branches have branches, and so on – just like a tree.

Darwin's Tree of Life sketch

Darwin drew this doodle in 1837, many years before he published his ideas. The sketch shows that he had already figured out an important part of how evolution works and how one species can become many. Though all life started from one living thing, new species branched off, over and over again. Not all the branches on the 'tree' kept going; some became extinct. But often, when one species split into two, both kept going and branching, evolving into different groups of living things.

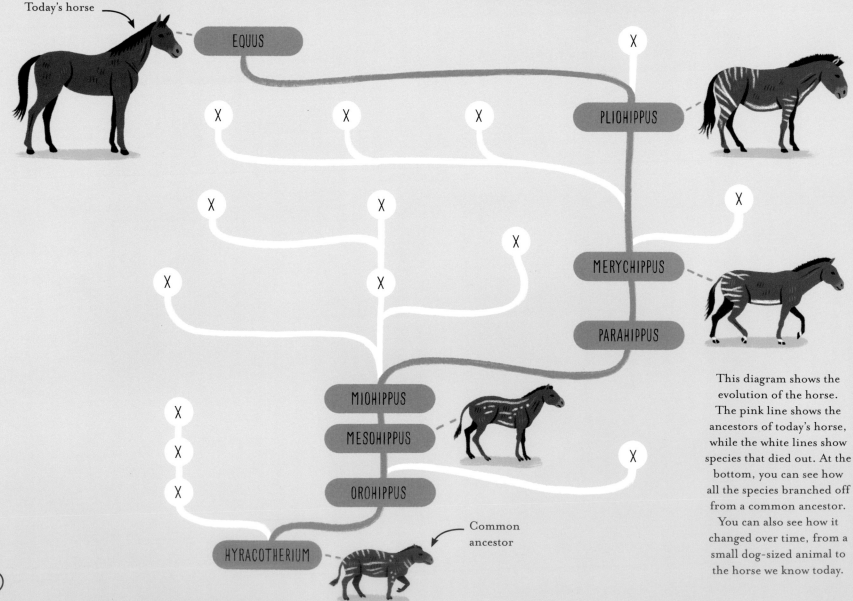

Today's horse

EQUUS

PLIOHIPPUS

MERYCHIPPUS

PARAHIPPUS

MIOHIPPUS

MESOHIPPUS

OROHIPPUS

HYRACOTHERIUM

Common ancestor

This diagram shows the evolution of the horse. The pink line shows the ancestors of today's horse, while the white lines show species that died out. At the bottom, you can see how all the species branched off from a common ancestor. You can also see how it changed over time, from a small dog-sized animal to the horse we know today.

IS ALL OF LIFE A TREE?

Scientists think all species evolved from one, single-celled life form. If that's right, then the whole of evolution could be shown as a tree diagram, with one single 'trunk'. If you could draw it all in detail, it would have to be huge, to show the millions of extinct and living species. It would also be much more complicated than a real tree.

OTHER SINGLE-CELLED LIFE FORMS

BACTERIA

MULTI-CELLED LIFE FORMS

Most types of living things are single-celled.

Animals are the most complex multi-celled life forms.

You might think of vertebrate animals, such as humans, cats, dogs, fish and birds, as 'normal' living things. But as the tree of life shows, they make up only a tiny fraction of the tree of life. Most of the tree's branches are taken up by single-celled creatures such as bacteria and amoebas. Scientists think there are many more single-celled species still to be discovered.

WHICH IS WHICH?

Scientists sort living things out into different groups, depending on their body parts, abilities, and genes and DNA. This sorting out process is called classification. For example, birds have feathers, but no other living things do. So, if an animal has feathers, it is classified as a bird.

SMALLER AND SMALLER GROUPS

A Swedish doctor and scientist, Carl Linnaeus, developed the classification system in the 1700s. Living things are divided into several main groups, such as animals, plants, fungi and bacteria. Each group can then be split into smaller groups, and these groups into even smaller groups, and so on. The large groups correspond to the big, main branches in the tree of life. The smaller groups are like the smaller branches and twigs, and the species at the end is like a single leaf on the tree.

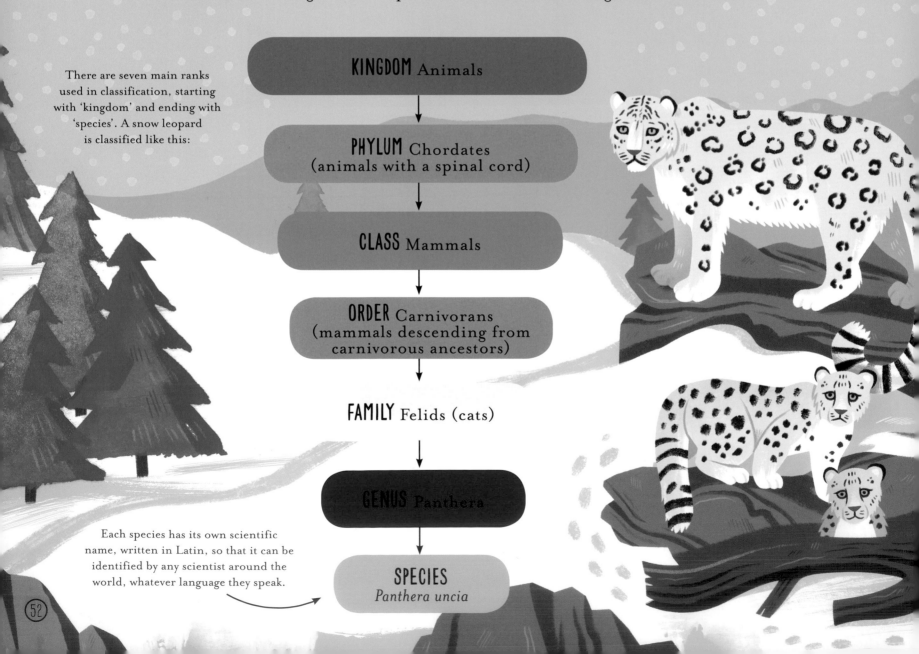

There are seven main ranks used in classification, starting with 'kingdom' and ending with 'species'. A snow leopard is classified like this:

KINGDOM Animals

PHYLUM Chordates
(animals with a spinal cord)

CLASS Mammals

ORDER Carnivorans
(mammals descending from carnivorous ancestors)

FAMILY Felids (cats)

GENUS Panthera

SPECIES
Panthera uncia

Each species has its own scientific name, written in Latin, so that it can be identified by any scientist around the world, whatever language they speak.

CLOSEST RELATIVES

As well as belonging to the whole 'tree of life', each species also has its own family tree, made up of its closest relatives – the branches nearest to it on the tree. When scientists are studying living things, they use family trees like this to show how animals are related. A living thing's closest relatives aren't always what you might expect …

Which animal is the closest relative of whales and dolphins? You can find out on this family tree.

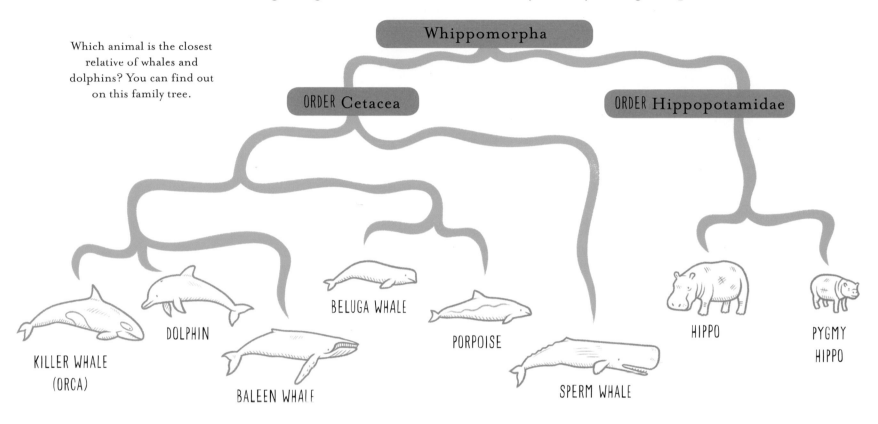

Whippomorpha

ORDER Cetacea

ORDER Hippopotamidae

KILLER WHALE (ORCA)

DOLPHIN

BALEEN WHALE

BELUGA WHALE

PORPOISE

SPERM WHALE

HIPPO

PYGMY HIPPO

ADDING TO THE TREE

When biologists discover a new species, they have to decide where in the tree of life it belongs, and how to classify it. They compare its features to other living things, and study its genes and DNA to see which other species it is most closely related to. Then they add it to the right branch of the tree.

The mimic octopus was discovered in Indonesia in 1998. It was added to the 'Octopodidae' family of octopuses.

MIMIC OCTOPUS

This amazing octopus can imitate other animals, such as the poisonous banded sole, in order to scare away predators.

BANDED SOLE

KINGDOM Animals

↓

PHYLUM Mollusc

↓

CLASS Cephalopod

↓

ORDER Octopoda

↓

FAMILY Octopodidae

↓

GENUS Thaumoctopus

↓

SPECIES
Thaumoctopus mimicus

CHAPTER 4

EVOLUTION IN ACTION

For some people, it's hard to believe that the slow, step-by-step process of evolution could have created some of the incredible features and abilities that living things have. How did evolution lead to the complex eyes of octopuses, dragonflies and humans, and the ability to see clearly? How could animals that crawled or ran on the ground evolve into flying animals with wings? And how could humans have evolved from their earliest ancestors into thinking, talking beings who can create all kinds of amazing inventions, from hammers and scissors to cookers, cars and computers?

Astonishing as it may seem, evolution can lead to these things, and many more amazing adaptations too.

EYE-VOLUTION

From tiny flies to eagle-eyed birds of prey and spectacle-wearing humans, most animals have eyes. Our planet is bathed in light from our nearest star, the Sun. The ability to see light means a living thing can detect the objects around it, even things that are far away. This helps animals to find food, hunt for prey, avoid danger, and seek out a mate.

HOW EYES EVOLVED

Basic light-sensing organs appeared early on in the history of animal life. They evolved into the many different types of eyes that animals have today.

① EYE SPOT, OR OCELLUS

The simplest eye is an eye spot, which is a patch of photoreceptors. These are cells that can detect the difference between light and dark, as they are sensitive to light energy.

EUGLENA (SINGLE-CELLED ORGANISM)

③ PRIMITIVE LENS

In a primitive lens eye, a curved clear layer evolved over the eye pit, helping the animal to see more clearly.

MARINE SNAIL

② EYE PIT

More complex than an eye spot is an eye pit, which has photoreceptors in a pit or hollow. This cuts out light from the sides, helping the animal to see better.

LIMPET

⑤ CAMERA LENS EYES

Primitive lens eyes evolved into camera lens eyes, like our own. These bend and focus light onto the light-sensitive retina at the back of the eye to make a clear, sharp image.

Separately from humans, octopuses evolved their own, different type of camera lens eye.

④ COMPOUND EYES

Compound eyes are made up of many lenses. House flies and dragonflies have large, complex compound eyes, containing thousands of lenses.

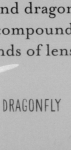

OCTOPUS

HUMAN

DRAGONFLY

HOW MANY EYES?

Many animals have two eyes, which gives them 3D vision. Each eye sees objects from a slightly different angle. This lets the brain work out things like how far away an object is, and how fast it's moving.

Spiders can have up to eight eyes. This wolf spider has two large 'seeing' eyes and six smaller eyes for sensing movement.

A bay scallop has over 100 bright blue eyes. They act like mirrors by directing light onto the scallop's light-sensitive retinas, helping it to spot tiny bits of food floating around it.

ENORMOUS EYES

Extra-large eyes evolve to help animals scan a wide area, or to see in dim light, such as at night or deep underwater.

At 5 cm in diameter, the ostrich's eyes are the largest of any land animal. They allow it to see predators from far away.

The biggest eyes in the animal kingdom belong to the colossal squid. Its eyes are up to 25 cm in diameter – wider than a football.

The tarsier lives in the rainforests of Southeast Asia and is nocturnal. Its bulging eyes are about the same size as its brain.

SENSING LIGHT

Plants don't have eyes, but they do have photoreceptors in their stems and leaves. This allows them to detect light and grow towards it.

INTO THE AIR

For thousands of years, humans watched flying animals in amazement, and wished they could fly too. Now we can, thanks to our ability to invent things, such as planes and hot-air balloons. But humans are nowhere near being able to fly on their own, like a bird, a bee or a bat can. How did these animals evolve the ability to take to the air?

FOUR FLYING GROUPS

Look at a bat, an eagle and a mosquito, and you'll see they all have very different wings, and fly in very different ways. This is because flying evolved separately in different animal groups. There was no single, early flying animal that evolved into all the fliers we have today. Instead, flying has evolved four times:

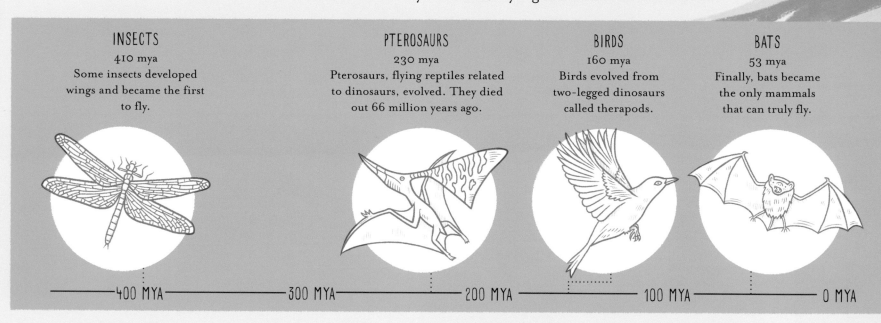

INSECTS
410 mya
Some insects developed wings and became the first to fly.

PTEROSAURS
230 mya
Pterosaurs, flying reptiles related to dinosaurs, evolved. They died out 66 million years ago.

BIRDS
160 mya
Birds evolved from two-legged dinosaurs called therapods.

BATS
53 mya
Finally, bats became the only mammals that can truly fly.

——400 MYA—— ——300 MYA—— ——200 MYA—— ——100 MYA—— ——0 MYA

- THE FIRST FLIERS -

Insects evolved flight an incredibly long time ago, and there are not many insect fossils to show how it happened. So it's still a puzzle for scientists. The main theory is that early insect wings evolved from large gills, found in some water insects.

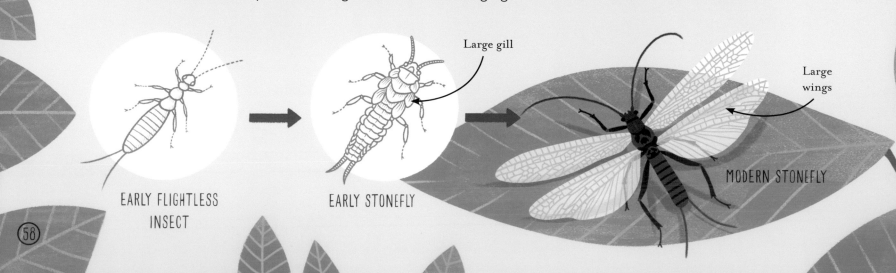

Large gill

Large wings

EARLY FLIGHTLESS INSECT

EARLY STONEFLY

MODERN STONEFLY

· EVOLUTION IN ACTION ·

- FLYING REPTILES -

Pterosaurs probably evolved from small land reptiles that moved around by running and hopping. They may have developed flaps of skin on their front limbs that helped them to leap, then glide and fly. As pterosaurs evolved, they grew bigger. They include the biggest-ever flying animals, such as *Quetzalcoatlus*. Pterosaurs became extinct in the K-T mass extinction 66 million years ago, along with the dinosaurs.

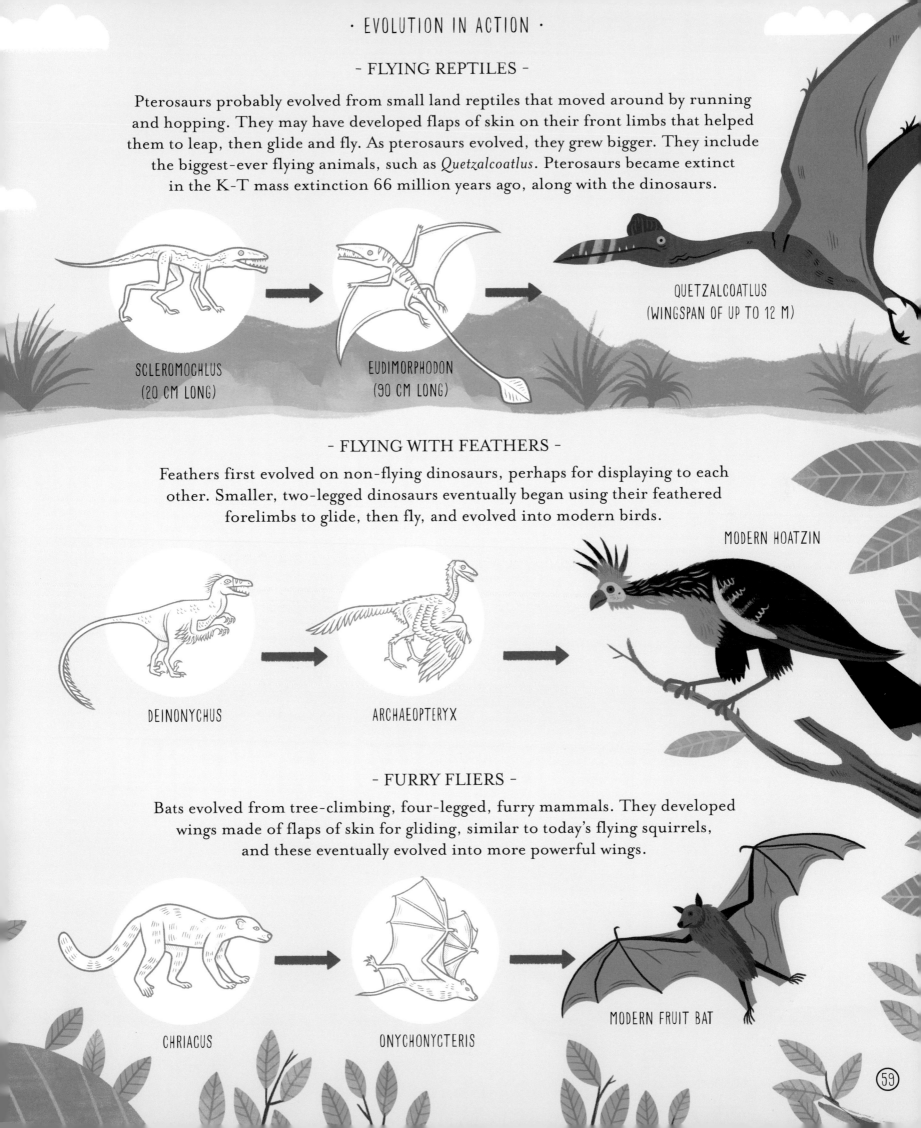

SCLEROMOCHLUS
(20 CM LONG)

EUDIMORPHODON
(90 CM LONG)

QUETZALCOATLUS
(WINGSPAN OF UP TO 12 M)

- FLYING WITH FEATHERS -

Feathers first evolved on non-flying dinosaurs, perhaps for displaying to each other. Smaller, two-legged dinosaurs eventually began using their feathered forelimbs to glide, then fly, and evolved into modern birds.

MODERN HOATZIN

DEINONYCHUS

ARCHAEOPTERYX

- FURRY FLIERS -

Bats evolved from tree-climbing, four-legged, furry mammals. They developed wings made of flaps of skin for gliding, similar to today's flying squirrels, and these eventually evolved into more powerful wings.

CHRIACUS

ONYCHONYCTERIS

MODERN FRUIT BAT

PLANTS AND POLLINATORS

For millions of years, some plants and animals have evolved to help each other survive. It's a brilliant example of co-evolution, where two living things evolve together in a way that is useful to them both.

HOW IT BEGAN

About 400 million years ago, the first seed plants evolved. To make seeds, male cells, called pollen, joined with cells in female plants – a process called 'pollination'. At first, pollen moved between plants by blowing in the wind, but over time, plants began to be pollinated by insects, too.

If an insect landed on a plant, pollen might brush off on it. When it landed on another plant, some pollen could get left there. In this way, insects could pollinate plants. This led to plants evolving features that attracted insects. If a plant species provided food, for example, more insects would visit and pollinate it. The species would make more seeds, and survive better.

Over time, plants evolved different flower shapes, colours, scents and other attractive features, such as making sugary nectar. Bees, which feed on nectar, are especially important pollinators.

Worker honeybees visit flowers to collect nectar and pollen. They use nectar to make honey, and pollen to feed their babies.

The flower's stamens produce pollen.

The bee collects bundles of pollen on her legs. More pollen sticks to her fur.

As the honeybee moves around, some pollen brushes off onto other flowers, and pollinates them.

POLLINATION PARTNERSHIPS

Bees aren't the only pollinators. Many other insects,
and other animals, have co-evolved with plants too.

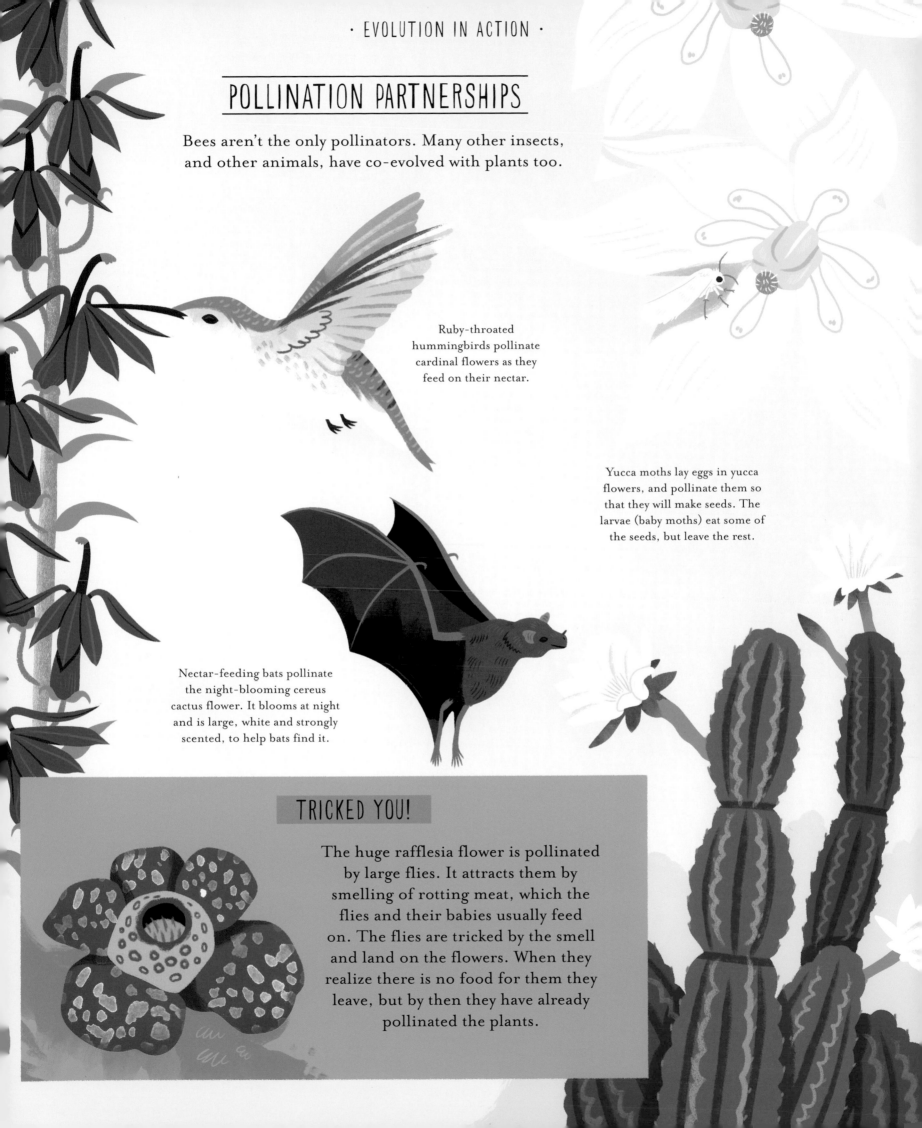

Ruby-throated
hummingbirds pollinate
cardinal flowers as they
feed on their nectar.

Yucca moths lay eggs in yucca
flowers, and pollinate them so
that they will make seeds. The
larvae (baby moths) eat some of
the seeds, but leave the rest.

Nectar-feeding bats pollinate
the night-blooming cereus
cactus flower. It blooms at night
and is large, white and strongly
scented, to help bats find it.

TRICKED YOU!

The huge rafflesia flower is pollinated
by large flies. It attracts them by
smelling of rotting meat, which the
flies and their babies usually feed
on. The flies are tricked by the smell
and land on the flowers. When they
realize there is no food for them they
leave, but by then they have already
pollinated the plants.

OUR BEST FRIENDS

Before modern humans came along, dogs such as labradors, poodles and terriers didn't exist. Pet dogs are a type of wolf that has evolved and adapted quite recently to live with humans.

MAKING FRIENDS

In prehistoric times, wolves were enemies of humans. They could be dangerous, and they hunted animals that humans relied on for food, such as deer. So people probably sometimes killed wolves, or scared them away.

At some point, perhaps as long as 30–40,000 years ago, some wolves began to live more closely with humans. No one is sure if it started with wolves entering human settlements, or with humans catching wolves and trying to train them. Maybe it was both. Humans and wolves both benefited from the relationship.

- GOOD FOR WOLVES -

If wolves followed humans, they could finish off their kills.

Wolves probably raided rubbish and bones from human villages.

Scary, aggressive wolves would be chased away. But a friendly, affectionate wolf might be allowed to stay.

- GOOD FOR HUMANS -

From watching wolves, humans could learn about tracking prey and hunting in groups. Maybe they started hunting alongside wolf packs and chose the friendliest wolves as hunting partners.

In villages, wolves that cleared up garbage, and got rid of other pests, like rats, would be useful.

A really friendly wolf might cuddle up to humans and keep them warm. Eventually, humans welcomed wolves into their homes.

EVOLVING INTO DOGS

Evolution happens when useful features help a species to survive. For a wolf living with humans, useful features would be:

- Friendly and affectionate
- Good at hunting
- Good at learning

Humans would keep wolves with these features, and help them to breed. Over time, wolves evolved into loving, loyal pet dogs. Selecting dogs with particular features, such as a good sense of smell or a waterproof coat, then created the many different dog breeds.

WORKING TOGETHER

Humans and dogs have been evolving together for thousands of years. This is why we have such a close relationship. Besides being companions, we train them to do all kinds of jobs for us, such as guiding blind people, helping the police, herding livestock and searching for earthquake survivors.

Dogs understand our words and signals.

Working dogs help humans.

We understand their barks and gestures, such as tail-wagging.

Humans and their dogs feel love and care for each other.

YOUR AMAZING BRAIN

Think about what you're doing right now. Looking at words on a page, understanding them, and thinking about what they mean. As far as we know, humans are the only living things that can do this, thanks to our super-powerful brains – one of the most amazing adaptations of all.

BRAIN POWER

Living things evolve features that help them to survive, like big claws, sharp thorns or the ability to fly. Humans are the same, but our most useful feature is our intelligence. We've evolved to survive by smartness, and by working together in groups.

This has resulted in us evolving the most complex brains of any animal. We use our brains to sense our surroundings, control our bodies, understand things, make decisions and think up ideas, and to store information and memories. We can also talk, helping us to transmit our knowledge and ideas to each other.

A human brain has around 90 billion brain cells, and trillions of connections linking them to each other.

USING TOOLS

When early humans began walking bipedally (on two legs), it freed up their hands for making things and using tools. Being good at making things gave these humans a survival advantage. They lived in groups, so it was also useful to be able to share ideas.

Two million years ago, the early hominin *Homo habilis* used stone tools to skin and butcher large animals.

Hunters worked together to track and bring down their prey.

THE GROWING BRAIN

Natural selection favoured smart humans who were good at using their hands, thinking up solutions to problems, and communicating their thoughts. Over time, this meant the brain evolved to become larger and more powerful.

Over millions of years, as the human brain increased in size, the human skull grew larger, too.

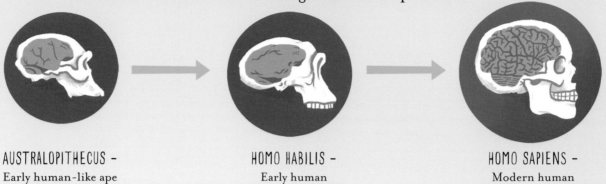

AUSTRALOPITHECUS –
Early human-like ape
(4 mya to 2 mya)

HOMO HABILIS –
Early human
(2.1 mya to 1.5 mya)

HOMO SAPIENS –
Modern human
(between 300,000 and 200,000 years ago to present)

More powerful brains helped us to make hunting tools, plan hunts, and catch more food, especially meat. We also learned to cook food, making meat easier to eat. This extra meat provided more protein and energy. In turn, this allowed the brain to evolve even more, as complex brains need a lot of protein and energy to grow and work. And, as the brain evolved, some areas became especially complex:

The section of the primary motor cortex that controls the small, detailed movements of the hands

Broca's area, used for words and language

The frontal lobe, used for planning, understanding and imagining

BIGHEADS?

Humans may be smart, but we don't have the biggest brains in the world. That honour goes to the sperm whale, whose brain is the size of a beach ball. But brain size alone isn't the most important thing when it comes to intelligence. These things matter more:

BRAIN SIZE COMPARED TO BODY SIZE
Human brains are much bigger than average for an animal of our size.

WRINKLINESS
The thinking part of the brain is the outer layer, or cortex. The more folds it has, the greater the surface area is and the more brain cells it has. So smarter animals have wrinklier brains!

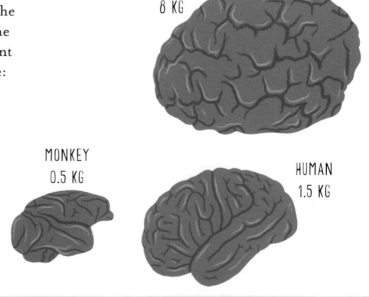

SPERM WHALE
8 KG

MONKEY
0.5 KG

HUMAN
1.5 KG

ARE WE STILL EVOLVING?

Evolution is still happening to living things around the world, including humans. As long as a species can reproduce, and has differences between individuals, it can evolve.

THE CHANGING MOTH

The peppered moth is a famous example of recent evolution. The peppered moth species has paler and darker varieties. Over several decades, the genes for darker wings became more common, and the species became mostly dark. This is how it happened:

①

Three hundred years ago, most peppered moths were pale coloured. This gave them good camouflage against the birch trees they rested on and protected them from predators.

②

Rarer, dark moths existed, too. They stood out against the birch and were easier for birds to find and eat.

③

In 19th-century Europe, more and more coal was burned as fuel. The soot made walls and tree trunks darker. Now darker moths had better camouflage than paler moths. Paler moths were easier for birds to catch.

④

More dark peppered moths survived to pass on their genes, and the species became mostly dark.

EVOLVING HUMANS

Humans take much longer than moths to grow up and have babies, so we evolve more slowly. However, scientists can study our genes to find out how they are changing. They show that we are evolving in several ways.

DRINKING MILK

Babies digest their mothers' milk using a body chemical called lactase. Long ago, in early humans, the body stopped making lactase in childhood. When people began farming milk animals, such as cattle, it was an advantage to be able to survive on dairy products. Gradually, in areas where this type of farming is common, most humans have evolved to make lactase as adults, and can now drink animals' milk.

WISDOM TEETH

Wisdom teeth are big chewing teeth that grow at the back of your mouth. Many people's mouths don't have space for them, and they have to be pulled out. In early humans, wisdom teeth helped us get nutrition from chewing raw food. Now, we eat mainly cooked and convenience food, and don't need wisdom teeth to survive. Our mouths are evolving to be smaller, and some people now don't grow wisdom teeth at all.

PROTECTIVE GENES

In places where many people are killed by the deadly disease malaria, genes that protect against the disease are becoming more common. Natural selection means that those people who have the helpful genes by chance are more likely to live longer, have children, and pass the useful genes on.

PLANTARIS MUSCLE

The plantaris muscle in the leg is used to help flex the feet. Some animals use it to grip things with their feet, but humans don't really need it at all. We have now begun to evolve towards losing this muscle, and about 10 per cent of people are born without it.

THE FUTURE FOR HUMANS

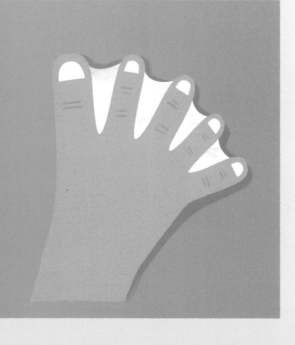

Scientists think that in the future, humans could evolve in various ways:

· As rising sea levels make the world more watery, we could become better at swimming and holding our breath, and might evolve webbed fingers and toes.

· We could become less muscly, as we don't need as much strength to survive in the modern world.

· Our bodies could evolve to get better at coping with sugar, a big part of modern diets.

AMAZING ADAPTATIONS
FACT FILE

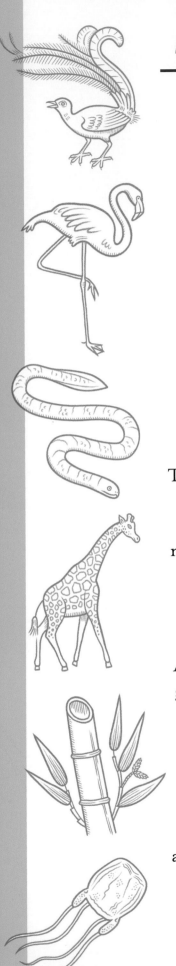

Many animals and plants have developed fascinating evolutionary features over the centuries. In this section, we look at some examples of the following:

- MICROORGANISMS -

Microorganisms are tiny, usually single-celled living things that you can only see with a microscope. The first life to evolve on Earth was single-celled. Today, there are thousands of species of bacteria and other microorganisms. Many of them are germs that can infect other living things and cause diseases, but others can be useful.

- PLANTS -

These life forms use light energy to make their food and grow, a process called photosynthesis. As plants don't have to hunt or look for food, they mainly stay in one place, rooted into the soil. Plants are vital for most animal life on Earth. They provide food for plant-eating animals, which in turn provide food for meat-eating animals. Without plants, there would certainly be no humans.

- FUNGI -

Although they are sometimes thought of as plants, fungi are a different group of living things, which do not need light to survive. Instead they grow and feed on other living or dead substances. Mushrooms and toadstools are fungi, but there are many other types too, including moulds and yeast.

- INVERTEBRATES -

Animals that don't have a backbone, or vertebral column, are known as invertebrates. Usually, they don't have bones at all, though some have shells, or a hard outer skin called an exoskeleton. They include many smaller animals like insects, worms and snails. But some invertebrates can grow quite big, especially sea creatures such as jellyfish and squid.

- FISH -

Almost all fish live mainly in water, and have gills for breathing underwater. They are vertebrates, and have backbones and skeletons. They use their fins, tails or both for swimming.

- AMPHIBIANS -

Amphibians, such as frogs, toads and salamanders, start their lives in the water. But after hatching out and growing, most amphibians develop lungs for breathing air, and can live partly on land. They return to the water to lay their eggs.

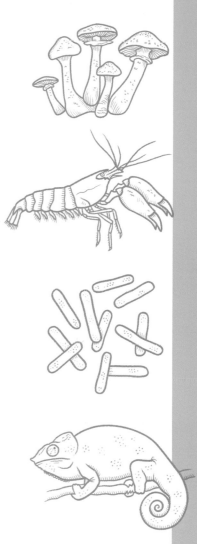

- REPTILES -

Reptiles are scaly, usually four-legged animals that include lizards, turtles and crocodiles. The dinosaurs and pterosaurs, which are now extinct, were also reptiles. Reptiles are mostly cold-blooded, so need to take heat from their surroundings to stay warm enough. That's why they are less common in colder parts of the world.

- BIRDS -

The most common of all vertebrates are birds. They have feathers, which can trap and resist air, giving the bird lift for flying, and insulation for warmth. Birds also have a beak, and lay eggs with hard shells. They are warm-blooded, meaning their bodies can make heat to keep them at the right temperature.

- MAMMALS -

These animals are warm-blooded and usually hairy or furry. They include many of the animals most familiar to us, such as dogs, mice, elephants and monkeys, and sea mammals, such as whales and dolphins. Mother mammals feed their babies on milk from their bodies.

MINDBOGGLING MICROORGANISMS

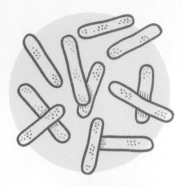

GUT BACTERIA

Billions of these bacteria live in your large intestine. Gut bacteria co-evolved with humans, feeding on fibre found in food, and making chemicals that help keep our bodies healthy.

MALARIA PARASITE

Plasmodium, a single-celled microorganism, has evolved to live inside mosquitoes. The insects pass it into humans in their bite, causing the deadly disease malaria.

FLU VIRUS

A virus is a tiny germ that has adapted to infect and live in other creatures. The flu virus causes the disease flu, or influenza.

PHENOMENAL PLANTS

GINKGO TREE (GINKGO BILOBA)

Ginkgo trees evolved 270 million years ago, and are brilliant survivors. Some even made it through the nuclear bomb blast that hit Hiroshima, Japan, in 1945.

BEE ORCHID (OPHRYS APIFERA)

This amazing orchid has evolved a flower that resembles a female bee. This attracts male bees, which pollinate the plant.

DODDER VINE (CUSCUTA)

The creepy dodder has evolved to survive by clinging to other plants and feeding on them. It can detect its favourite prey plants by their smell, and grows towards them.

BAMBOO (BAMBUSOIDEAE)

Bamboos are members of the grass family that have evolved to grow to a huge size. Some species can grow incredibly fast: up to 90 cm in a single day!

CALIFORNIA REDWOOD (SEQUOIA SEMPERVIRENS)

This enormous evergreen tree grows taller than any other, reaching up to 115 m high. It can live for over 2,000 years, and has adapted to regrow itself if damaged by fire.

FABULOUS FUNGI

RED CAGE FUNGUS (CLATHRUS RUBER)

This amazing toadstool is shaped like a red cage or basket. It stinks of rotting meat to attract flies and beetles, which help to spread its spores and grow more fungi.

HUMONGOUS FUNGUS (ARMILLARIA OSTOYAE)

Many fungi grow in clusters, linked underground by roots called mycelium. In Oregon, USA, a single honey fungus spreads across 9 square kilometres, and is nicknamed the 'humongous fungus'.

BAKER'S YEAST (SACCHAROMYCES CEREVISIAE)

The yeast used in breadmaking is a type of single-celled fungus which has adapted to feed on sugar. It releases carbon dioxide gas as it feeds, which makes bread dough rise.

INCREDIBLE INVERTEBRATES

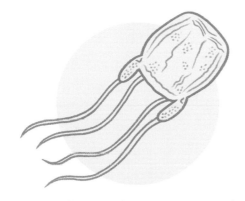

BOX JELLYFISH (CHIRONEX FLECKERI)

The box jellyfish or 'sea wasp' has developed the most powerful venom of any animal. It uses it to kill prey and to defend against predators.

TARDIGRADE (TARDIGRADA)

Tiny tardigrades are super-survivors that have adapted amazing resistance to extreme heat and cold, starvation, drying out, poison, nuclear radiation, and even the vacuum of outer space.

HIMALAYAN JUMPING SPIDER (EUOPHRYS OMNISUPERSTES)

Adapted to live at altitudes of up to 6,700 m, the tiny Himalayan jumping spider may be the world's highest-dwelling animal. It eats insects that are blown up from lower slopes.

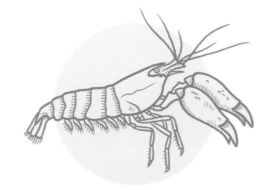

MONARCH BUTTERFLY (DANAUS PLEXIPPUS)

Every year in North America, millions of monarch butterflies migrate huge distances back to the tree where their great-great-grandparents hatched out – but no one has worked out how they know where to go.

PISTOL SHRIMP (ALPHEIDAE)

Tiny pistol shrimps make one of the loudest noises in the sea by snapping the pincers on a large, specially adapted claw. The blast of sound kills or stuns small fish.

COMMON OCTOPUS (OCTOPUS VULGARIS)

The common octopus has evolved the ability to change its skin colour, texture and shape in seconds, allowing it to disguise itself as sand, rocks or seaweed.

FASCINATING FISH

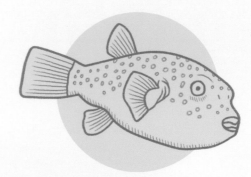

HAGFISH (MYXINI)

The hagfish has evolved a useful defence against predators. It releases chemicals that turn the water into thick, stringy slime, clogging predators' mouths and gills. It then ties itself in a knot, which it runs along its body to wipe the slime off!

FLYING FISH (EXOCOETIDAE)

Flying fish have fins that have evolved to work like wings. If in danger, they leap out of the water and zoom through the air, covering distances of up to 400 m.

WHITE-SPOTTED PUFFERFISH (TORQUIGENER ALBOMACULOSUS)

The male white-spotted pufferfish uses his body to create circular patterns on the sandy seabed. If a female likes the circle, she lays her eggs there. It's a kind of sexual selection, as the males who make the best circles get to have babies and pass on their genes.

BARRELEYE (MACROPINNA MICROSTOMA)

The bizarre barreleye has large, tube-shaped eyes that can point upwards or forwards, enclosed in a clear dome on its head! This helps it to check a wide area for prey, while protecting its eyes.

PEACOCK FLOUNDER (BOTHUS MANCUS)

The peacock flounder is famous for its camouflage. It can change colour to match a sandy seabed, rocks or coral. In scientific tests, it even managed to match a black-and-white checkerboard pattern.

SEAHORSE (HIPPOCAMPUS)

Seahorses are fish, but have evolved an upright body and a horse-like head. The female lays her eggs in a pouch on the male's body, and he keeps the eggs until they hatch.

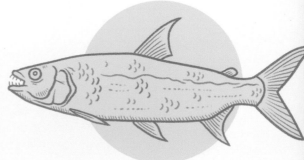

GIANT MANTA RAY (MANTA BIROSTRIS)

The 'wings' of the giant manta ray can grow to 7 m across. Despite being so huge, these rays can propel themselves out of the water and high into the air – possibly a way of signalling to each other.

ICEFISH (NOTOTHENIOIDEI)

Icefish live in cold waters around Antarctica. They look almost transparent, and their blood is clear, as they have no red blood cells. Scientists think this may be due to an accidental genetic mutation.

AFRICAN TIGERFISH (HYDROCYNUS)

Tigerfish are big, fierce fish that live in African rivers and lakes. They feed mostly on smaller fish, but some have developed the ability to leap out of the water to grab birds from mid-air.

AMAZING AMPHIBIANS

GOLDEN POISON FROG
(PHYLLOBATES TERRIBILIS)

The golden poison frog from Colombia, South America, is one of the world's most toxic animals. Like many poisonous animals, it has evolved 'warning colouration' – bright colours that act as a warning to predators.

CHINESE GIANT SALAMANDER
(ANDRIAS DAVIDIANUS)

This river-dweller is the world's biggest amphibian, with a maximum length of 1.8 m. It feeds on smaller water animals, and has evolved the ability to sense their movements through its skin.

AFRICAN GIANT TOAD
(AMIETOPHRYNUS SUPERCILIARIS)

This large toad lives around forest riverbanks in central Africa, and has evolved brilliant camouflage that resembles a fallen leaf.

REMARKABLE REPTILES

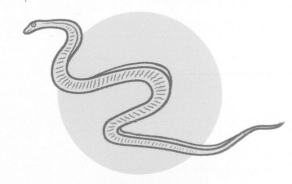

FLYING SNAKE (CHRYSOPELEA)

In the forests of southeast Asia, flying snakes climb trees using ridges on their undersides, and glide from the high branches by flattening out their bodies and 'swimming' through the air.

SEA SNAKE (HYDROPHIINAE)

Sea snakes have evolved to live in seas and oceans. They have paddle-shaped tails for swimming, and come to the surface to breathe air. Some, such as Belcher's sea snake, have extremely deadly venom.

EASTERN LONG-NECKED TURTLE
(CHELODINA LONGICOLLIS)

This Australian turtle has evolved a long, snake-like neck that can be even longer than its body. It keeps it folded inside its shell as it looks for food, then darts it out to grab its prey.

SALTWATER CROCODILE (CROCODYLUS POROSUS)

Unlike most crocodiles, the saltwater crocodile has adapted to swim in salty ocean estuaries or even out at sea. 'Salties' can hunt and eat sharks, deer, kangaroos, cows and even tigers.

CHAMELEON (CHAMAELEONIDAE)

Chameleons have evolved pincer-shaped feet for gripping branches, and long, sticky tongues that can suddenly shoot out to catch prey. Their eyes can rotate to give them 360-degree vision.

TOKAY GECKO (GEKKO GECKO)

Geckos are famous for their ability to climb almost any surface, even glass. Their large toes are covered in millions of tiny hairs called setae, which latch onto the surface.

BRILLIANT BIRDS

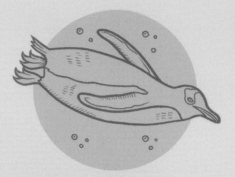

CASSOWARY (CASUARIUS)

Large flightless birds like ostriches and cassowaries are the birds most closely related to reptiles. The cassowary's body shape and big, scaly feet resemble a two-legged dinosaur such as a *Velociraptor*.

CUCKOO (CUCULIDAE)

The cuckoo has evolved to trick another bird into bringing up its chick. It lays an egg in the other bird's nest, pushing the bird's own egg out. The bird then feeds the baby cuckoo when it hatches – even when it grows larger than its foster parents.

GENTOO PENGUIN (PYGOSCELIS PAPUA)

Penguins are seabirds. They can't fly, but their wings have evolved into flippers that work like wings underwater. The gentoo penguin can reach speeds of over 35 km per hour.

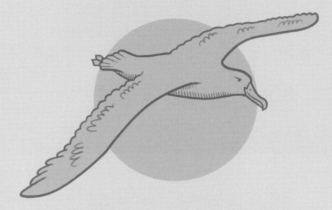

TURKEY VULTURE (CATHARTES AURA)

Vultures feed on the remains of dead animals. Their bald heads have evolved to help them reach inside a carcass without getting their feathers dirty, and may also help them to cool off in the heat.

WANDERING ALBATROSS (DIOMEDEA EXULANS)

This huge white seabird has the longest wingspan of any bird – up to 3.5 m. Its long, slender wings make it a brilliant glider. It can stay out at sea for months or years, flying thousands of kilometres in search of food, and resting on the sea surface.

LYREBIRD (MENURA)

The Australian lyrebird is famous for mimicking other birds, animals and even human-made sounds. Males have evolved this ability through sexual selection. The best mimics are more likely to win a mate.

GREATER FLAMINGO (PHOENICOPTERUS ROSEUS)

Flamingos have evolved amazingly long, skinny legs, which they use to stand in shallow water in lakes, estuaries, swamps and lagoons. They feed with their heads upside-down in the water.

AFRICAN GREY PARROT (PSITTACUS ERITHACUS)

The large African grey parrot is highly intelligent and brilliant at learning human words. One parrot named Alex learned over 100 words and could understand numbers and colours too.

ZEBRA FINCH (TAENIOPYGIA GUTTATA)

Zebra finches are songbirds from Australia and Southeast Asia. The young male learns his song from his father or other adult males, and adds his own variations, so the songs themselves evolve over time.

MARVELLOUS MAMMALS

GIRAFFE (GIRAFFA)

The giraffe's long neck evolved because it gave it an advantage for reaching food on high tree branches. Though a giraffe's neck can be over 2 m long, it is made up of just seven bones, like a human's.

PLATYPUS (ORNITHORHYNCHUS ANATINUS)

The platypus is a monotreme, an unusual type of mammal that lays eggs. When the babies hatch, the mother feeds them with milk, like other mammals. Unlike most mammals, the platypus has a beak.

JERBOA (DIPODIDAE)

By convergent evolution, this Asian desert animal has evolved a similar body shape to the kangaroo, with big back legs for hopping, and a long tail for balance. It has also adapted to survive without drinking water, getting all its liquid by eating plants.

AYE-AYE (DAUBENTONIA MADAGASCARIENSIS)

The aye-aye from Madagascar, Africa, is a type of small lemur. It has evolved extra long, skinny middle fingers on each hand, which it uses to hook grubs (baby insects) out of holes in trees.

MEXICAN FREE-TAILED BAT (TADARIDA BRASILIENSIS)

Bats are the only mammals that have evolved the ability to fly. The Mexican free-tailed bat lives in huge colonies. It hunts using echolocation, making sounds and detecting the echoes that bounce off its prey.

ORCA (ORCINUS ORCA)

The orca is one of several types of mammal that has evolved to live in the sea. It breathes air using adapted nostrils, or blowholes, on its head. Orcas are very intelligent and communicate using popping and whistling sounds.

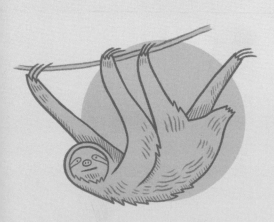

THREE-TOED SLOTH (BRADYPUS)

Sloths, from Central and South America, are famous for moving slowly, which helps them save energy. They often look greenish, thanks to algae that has co-evolved to grow in their fur, providing camouflage.

KOALA (PHASCOLARCTOS CINEREUS)

Koalas, from Australia, are marsupials: mammals that keep their newborn babies in a pouch of skin on their underside. They have adapted to eat eucalyptus leaves, which are toxic to other animals.

SNOW LEOPARD (PANTHERA UNCIA)

The snow leopard lives in the snowy mountains of central Asia. It has evolved thick fur to protect against the cold, even on its feet, and its grey and cream markings give it perfect camouflage.

 # GLOSSARY

ADAPT To change to suit new or changed surroundings or conditions.

AMBER FOSSIL A fossil preserved in amber, or fossilized tree resin.

AMOEBA A type of very simple, single-celled animal.

AMPHIBIAN A type of vertebrate animal that lays eggs in water, such as frogs and newts.

APE A branch of primates which includes gorillas, chimpanzees, orangutans, gibbons and humans.

AQUATIC Relating to or found in water.

ASTEROID Small rocky object that orbits the Sun, and can sometimes hit Earth.

BACTERIA Very small, single-celled microorganisms, found in almost every habitat.

BIOLOGY The study of living things.

CAMOUFLAGE Body shape, colour or pattern that helps a living thing to hide by matching its surroundings.

CELLS The tiny units that living things are made up of. Single-celled living things have only one cell each.

CLASSIFICATION The process of sorting living things into a system of types and groups.

CLIMATE The typical weather conditions in a particular place or area.

CO-EVOLUTION The evolution of two or more species to depend on or benefit from each other.

COLONY A group of animals, such as honeybees, that live together and help each other to survive.

COMPETITION Two or more living things or species trying to get more food, mates or other resources than each other.

COMPOUND EYE A type of animal eye made up of many separate mini-eyes.

CONSERVATION Efforts to protect and preserve living species and natural habitats.

CONVERGENT EVOLUTION The evolution of two or more species from different groups to look similar and behave in similar ways.

CORTEX The outer layer of the brain, used for sensing and processing information.

DIGITS Fingers or finger-like body parts on an animal's front limbs.

DNA (DEOXYRIBONUCLEIC ACID) A chemical found in cells, which contains the instructions that make the cell work.

ECOSYSTEM A community of living things and the habitat or surroundings they live in.

EON A very large division of geologic time, such as the Hadean Eon.

ERA A medium-length division of geologic time, such as the Mesozoic Era.

EVOLUTION A process of gradual change over multiple generations of living things.

EXOSKELETON A stiff protective outer covering or shell, found in animals such as insects and crabs.

EXTINCT No longer existing, having died out as a species.

FOSSIL The remains or trace of a prehistoric living thing, preserved in rock.

FOSSIL RECORD The fossils found so far and the way they are distributed in layers of rock, revealing how old each fossil is.

GENES Sequences of chemicals arranged along strands of DNA, which act as coded instructions for cells.

GENOME The full set of genes and DNA found in a particular living thing or species.

GEOLOGIC TIME The timescale of the whole history of the Earth, its rocks and life forms.

GILLS Breathing organs found in fish and some amphibians, which allow them to extract oxygen from water.

HABITAT The natural home or environment of a living thing or species.

HOMININ A modern human or a human ancestor, including all of the *Homo* species and the *Australopithecus* species.

ICHTHYOSAUR A type of prehistoric sea reptile which looked similar to a fish.

INVERTEBRATE An animal without a backbone.

KIN SELECTION The natural selection of colonies or families of living things, rather than of individuals.

LENS A clear part inside some types of animal eye, that bends and focuses rays of light that pass through it.

MAMMAL A type of vertebrate animal that feeds its young on milk from the mother's body.

MARSUPIAL A type of mammal that carries its babies in a pouch on the mother's underside.

MASS EXTINCTION The extinction of an unusually large number of species over a short period of time.

MICROORGANISM A very small living thing that we can only see using a microscope.

MIGRATE To travel long distances according to the seasons, usually to find food or a mate.

MINERALS Pure, natural, non-living substances, such as metals, quartz and silicon.

MOLECULE A group of two or more atoms.

MUTATION An accidental change that can occur when DNA is being copied between cells, causing differences between living things.

MYA An abbreviation for 'million years ago', often used to describe prehistoric dates or living things.

MYCELIUM A network of root-like hairs grown by a fungus to help it feed.

NATURALIST Someone who studies nature and living things.

NATURAL SELECTION The way living things that are better suited to their natural surroundings are 'selected' by nature to survive for longer and reproduce more than others.

NECTAR A sugary liquid made inside flowers to attract insects and other animals to pollinate a plant.

NICHE A particular position or role within an ecosystem.

NOCTURNAL Active at night.

PALAEONTOLOGY The study of fossils and what they reveal about prehistoric life.

PARASITE A living thing that lives in or on another living thing, without giving anything in return.

PERIODS Shorter divisions of geologic time, such as the Jurassic Period.

PHOTORECEPTOR A light-sensing cell or organ found in a living thing.

PLACENTAL MAMMAL A mammal that grows its babies inside the mother's body, feeding them using an organ called the placenta.

POLLEN Yellow powder released from flowers, containing male plant cells that are needed to make seeds.

POLLINATION The process of spreading pollen from one flower to another, so that flowering plants can make seeds.

PREDATOR An animal that hunts and eats other animals.

PREHISTORIC Dating from the time before people began to write down historic records.

PREY An animal that is hunted and eaten by another animal.

PRIMATE A type of furry mammal with flexible hands and feet and good eyesight, including monkeys, chimpanzees and humans.

PROTEIN A type of chemical found in living things, and used to build body parts and tissues.

PTEROSAUR A type of prehistoric flying reptile, with wings made from stretched skin.

REPRODUCTION The way species of living things make copies of themselves, for example by having babies or releasing seeds.

REPTILE A type of vertebrate animal that usually has scales, breathes air and lays eggs.

SAUROPODS A group of very large, four-legged, plant-eating dinosaurs with long necks and tails.

SELECTIVE BREEDING The process of choosing the most useful plants and animals to breed as farm animals and crops, making them evolve over time.

SEXUAL SELECTION A type of evolution that selects the individuals which are best at impressing and winning a mate, and are therefore more likely to reproduce.

SPECIATION The process of new species developing and branching off from previous species.

SPECIES A particular type of living thing, given its own two-part scientific name. Members of a species typically only reproduce with other members of the same species.

SPECIMEN A sample of a type of living thing, usually collected from the wild in order to study it.

SPIRACLES Breathing holes that some types of animals, such as insects and spiders, have on their bodies.

STRATA Layers of rock formed and laid down over time, with the oldest rocks in the deepest layers.

STROMATOLITE A mound-shaped or sheet-shaped fossil, formed by layers of prehistoric bacteria, and mud and sand trapped between them.

SUBSPECIES Different varieties or types of living things within one species.

TETRAPOD A type of four-legged vertebrate animal that evolved from early fish, and evolved into amphibians, reptiles, birds and mammals.

TRACE FOSSIL A fossil of an imprint or mark left by a living thing, such as a dinosaur footprint.

VARIATION The differences between different individual living things thanks to differences in their genes and DNA, even within the same species.

VERTEBRATE An animal with a backbone.

VIRUS A type of tiny germ, much smaller than most bacteria, which reproduces by invading the cells of living things.

INDEX

First published in the UK in 2019 by

Ivy Kids

An imprint of The Quarto Group
The Old Brewery
6 Blundell Street
London N7 9BH
United Kingdom
www.QuartoKnows.com

British Library Cataloguing-in-Publication Data
A catalogue record for this book is available from the British Library.

ISBN: 978-1-78240-636-5

This book was conceived, designed & produced by

Ivy Kids

58 West Street, Brighton BN1 2RA, United Kingdom

PUBLISHER Susan Kelly
CREATIVE DIRECTOR Michael Whitehead
MANAGING EDITOR Susie Behar
ART DIRECTOR Hanri van Wyk
DESIGNER Suzie Harrison
IN-HOUSE DESIGNER Kate Haynes
PROJECT EDITOR Claire Saunders
IN-HOUSE EDITOR Hannah Dove
CONSULTANT Dr Isabelle De Groote
ASSISTANT EDITOR Lucy Menzies

Manufactured in Guangdong, China CC012019

1 3 5 7 9 10 8 6 4 2

MIX
Paper from
responsible sources
FSC® C008047